A Kind of Love Story

By **Jenelle Riley**

STEELE SPRING STAGE RIGHTS

www.stagerights.com

A KIND OF LOVE STORY
Copyright © 2014 by Jenelle Riley
All Rights Reserved

All performances and public readings of A KIND OF LOVE STORY are subject to royalties. It is fully protected under the copyright laws of the United States of America, of all countries covered by the International Copyright Union, of all countries covered by the Pan-American Copyright Convention and the Universal Copyright Convention, and all countries with which the United States has reciprocal copyright relations. All rights are strictly reserved.

No part of this book may be reproduced, stored in a retrieval system, or transmitted in any form, by any means, including mechanical, electronic, photocopying, recording, or otherwise, without the prior written permission of the author. Publication of this play does not necessarily imply that it is available for performance by amateurs or professionals. It is strongly recommended all interested parties apply to Steele Spring Stage Rights for performance rights before starting rehearsals or advertising.
No changes shall be made in the play for the purpose of your production without prior written consent. All billing stipulations in your license agreement must be strictly adhered to. No person, firm or entity may receive credit larger or more prominent than that accorded the Author.

For all stage performance inquiries, please contact:

STEELE SPRING STAGE RIGHTS

Steele Spring Stage Rights
3845 Cazador Street
Los Angeles, CA 90065 (323) 739-0413
www.stagerights.com

PRODUCTION HISTORY

A Kind of Love Story had its world premiere at Sacred Fools Theatre in Los Angeles on September 21, 2012 with the following cast:

Michael Lanahan as "Mark"
Carrie Wiita as "Ally"
Curt Bonnem as "Bob"
Carrie Keranen as "Diane"
Erin Matthews as "Lucy"
Jennifer Christina Smith as "Kelly"
Rick Steadman as "Max"
Donelle Fuller, Will McMichael & Terry Tocantins – Ensemble
Eric Giancoli as "Narrator"

Understudies:
Anthony Backman as "Mark"/Ensemble
Bailee DesRocher as "Ally"/"Kelly"
Pete Caslavka as "Max"
Terry Tocantins as "Bob"
Lena Bouton as "Casey"/"Diane"/"Belle"
Emily Clark as "Lucy"/Ensemble

Producers: JJ Mayes, Ben Rock & Monica Greene
Associate Producers: Annette Fasone & Addi Gaash
Assistant Director: Bryan Bellomo
Stage Manager: Megan Crockett
Sound Design: Mark McClain Wilson
Lighting Design: Brandon Baruch
Set Design: Tifanie McQueen
Costume Design: Marianne Davis
Prop Design: Lisa Anne Nicolai
Projection Design: Anthony Backman
Graphic Design: Curt Bonnem
Title Card & Book Cover Illustrations: Amy Martinez
Photography: Jessica Sherman

CAST OF CHARACTERS

Cast Total: 11 – 6F, 4M, 1 Narrator

All characters are open to all ethnicities, ages 25-40.

MARK: Male lead. A born romantic, he's the nice guy who never gets the girl; kind, generous, intelligent.

ALLY: Female lead. Unlucky in love and put-upon, she is smart, funny, and good-natured.

LUCY: Ally's roommate; smarter than she lets on, charismatic but immature.

MAX: Ally's awful boyfriend; turns on the charm when he needs to, but usually boorish.

BOB: Mark's best friend; generally a good guy, he's been married to Diane for 10 years and is feeling restless.

DIANE: Bob's patient wife, Mark's dream girl; the classic girl next door.

CASEY/FEMALE ENSEMBLE: Famous lesbian activist and writer; beautiful, charismatic.

KELLY/FEMALE ENSEMBLE: Ally's no-nonsense best friend and the only woman who terrifies Max.

MALE ENSEMBLE: Plays a variety of characters, from Superman to Mark's father to various guys Ally flirts with.

FEMALE ENSEMBLE: Plays a variety of women Mark dates and ancillary characters.

NARRATOR: Male or female, all-knowing.

SETTING

Modern day, a big city

APPROXIMATE RUN TIME

1 hour and 45 minutes, with intermission

AUTHOR'S NOTES FOR PUBLICATION

A Kind of Love Story came to life through a late-night play series called *Serial Killers* at Sacred Fools Theatre in Los Angeles, though its origin probably goes back to childhood. For as long as I can remember, even before seeing *Sleepless in Seattle* as a kid, I've been fascinated with the concepts of destiny and coincidence.

Though I've been writing since I was five years old, I have always tended to hide behind my work. I avoided sentiment, thinking I needed to write dark or "edgy" comedy to win people over. But I was always a secret romantic, raised on rom-coms and fairy tales. My original plan with *A Kind of Love Story* was to mock romantic comedy conventions, making fun of the tropes we've all come to know and love. That's what I began with when I entered the first chapter at *Serial Killers*, a show that allows playwrights to present short snippets of a story every week; the audience votes on the pieces and the winning stories continue the following week. When I first premiered *A Kind of Love Story*, I thought it would get a few laughs and maybe run a couple weeks. But the secret sap, who had been hiding all these years, began to come out. And as it continued, I found people more invested in these characters than in any I'd ever written. And their investment allowed me to explore an unabashed romantic side that I had never fully allowed myself to give in to, for fear that I would be labelled maudlin or sentimental. The result was a show that ran through the rest of the season and went on to have its world premiere as a play at the very theatre where it began.

In the end it is my hope that the play has it both ways: both parodying and paying homage to the romantic comedy genre. Because everybody loves a happy ending.

ACT I

SCENE 1

Pre-show, a montage of love scenes from famous television shows and films is projected against the back wall. It makes up all mediums and genres— we see couples like Romeo and Juliet, Ozzie and Harriet, Fred and Wilma Flintstone. Kisses from "From Here to Eternity" to "Titanic." A YouTube clip of otters holding hands. As the show starts, we fade to black.

Melancholy music plays in the blackness.

VIDEO: A thick volume bound in leather opens to the first page.

TITLE CARD: "Prologue: A Boy and Girl."

NARRATOR: This is the story of two people who were made for each other. True soulmates. A man and a woman destined to fall madly in love with each other— if only they could ever meet.

> *The lights rise on a simple set of sparse platforms. The action on stage left will represent Allly's world, while stage right will represent Mark's world. ALLY enters.*

This is Allison O'Neill, Ally to her friends. Ally O. to family. She doesn't have any enemies, but if she did, they would probably call her Allison. Just to spite her.

> *ALLY reacts to what the NARRATOR is saying throughout the following:*

Ally goes by Allison only when speaking on the phone with strangers, otherwise the person she's talking to thinks she said "Sally." She loves the beach, thinks sushi is overrated, and giggles uncontrollably whenever she sees an unfixed Great Dane.

> *ALLY giggles.*

Ally is a dying breed in today's jaded times. Not a hopeless romantic, but a hopeful one. For as long as she can remember, she has wanted to be in love. At the age of seven, she set about getting her first kiss.

> *A YOUNG BOY walks out and up to ALLY. He sighs. Ally, behaving like a 7-year-old, shyly hands him a dollar.*

BOY: All right, just get it over with.

> *ALLY kisses him. The BOY wipes his face and makes disgusted noises. He exits. He quickly returns, and pushes Ally down before exiting.*

NARRATOR: Sadly, things did not improve much for Ally over the years. Age 17.

> *The BOY re-enters.*

BOY: Babe. I'd love to go out but I'm broke. Can you spring for pizza?

ALLY: Of course.

BOY: Great, I'll tell the rest of the team!

> *He races offstage.*

NARRATOR: Age 22.

> *The BOY re-enters.*

BOY: What's... "rent"?

ALLY: Nothing. I'll take care of it.

> *He exits.*

NARRATOR: Age 27.

> *The BOY enters. Before he can say anything:*

ALLY: Here's my ATM card and the keys to my apartment.

> *The lights slowly fade on ALLY as they rise stage left on MARK, guileless and open-faced.*

NARRATOR: Somewhere, across the very same city, Ally's true love was waiting for her. He just didn't know it yet. His name is Mark Collins. Mark always felt "Mark Collins" was a generic name, and could be used to describe anyone. So he made it his life's mission to be more interesting than his name.

> *MARK reacts to what the NARRATOR is saying throughout the following:*

The word most generally used to describe Mark is "nice." As in: "He's a nice guy." Always said with that inflection, as if it's a disease he's not quite over. Mark can spend an entire weekend reading in bed, sought-after Dungeon Master, and can't masturbate in his own room because he's afraid his goldfish is watching. Over the years, Mark had also developed a pattern with the ladies. Age 12.

> *A GIRL enters, looks at MARK apologetically.*

GIRL: I'm sorry, I just think of you as a friend.

> *MARK sags a bit as she exits.*

NARRATOR: Age 16.

> *The GIRL enters, excited.*

GIRL: Hey Mark, thanks for taking me out. I wanted you to fill me in on everything I could ever want to know about your cute friend Jimmy!

> *MARK sags again, as the GIRL exits.*

NARRATOR: Ages 22 through 31.

> *The GIRL enters, sobbing.*

GIRL: Can you stay up with me all night talking about how badly all my boyfriends treat me?

> *She cries on his shoulder.*

MARK: Of course! If I just hang in there and be a good friend, you're bound to fall in love with me eventually! This always works!

GIRL: What?

> *MARK pushes her head back down.*

MARK: Nothing. Ssh...

NARRATOR: But eventually, no matter how much they tried to acquiesce, they always ended up the same: alone.

> *The BOY and GIRL spot each other from opposite ends of the stage.*

BOY: Hey.

GIRL: Hey.

BOY: You wanna...

GIRL: Yeah!

> *They exit together. ALLY and MARK hang their heads.*

NARRATOR: For some people, love comes easy. Ally and Mark have never been those people. Part of the problem might have been expectations. For Ally, her ideals of love and romance are the result of being raised by a steady diet of Disney movies and Harlequin Romance novels. She didn't have the best people to turn to for advice.

> *BELLE, the heroine from "Beauty and the Beast," enters. ALLY is not surprised to see her.*

BELLE *(sing-song)*: Why, Ally, you look positively glum! What's wrong?

ALLY: Oh, hey Belle. I'm just wondering if the right guy is out there for me.

BELLE: I can understand it must be hard to see everyone else so happy. And here you are, all alone and closing in on 40.

ALLY: What? I'm 29!

BELLE *(laughing)*: Of course you are, dear!

> *BELLE winks and nudges her as the lights fade stage left and rise stage right:*

NARRATOR: For his part, Mark wasn't much better off. His main influences in the field of romance came from comic books and Cameron Crowe movies.

> *SUPERMAN enters, carrying a boom box above his head blasting "In Your Eyes."*

SUPERMAN: GREETINGS, CITIZEN!

MARK: Hey, Supe. 'Sup?

> *MARK chuckles at his little joke.*

SUPERMAN: Oh, Mark! You're always so clever for a human!

> *SUPERMAN slaps him on the back, which causes MARK to wince in pain.*

SUPERMAN: Now tell me, chum: why so blue?

MARK: I just don't know why I can't meet someone special. What am I doing wrong?

SUPERMAN: Why, I can't imagine either, Mark! It's so easy. I find a simple introduction works. "Hi, I'm Superman." That usually does the trick.

MARK: It doesn't really work that way for me, Superman.

SUPERMAN: Well, Mark, sometimes girls require what we Kryptonians call "a grand gesture."

MARK: Like sending flowers? Or serenading her with a song? I've done all that.

SUPERMAN: Hm. Hm. Hm. How about reversing the earth's rotation to turn back time? Have you done that, Mark?

MARK: ...no.

SUPERMAN: Well. Sounds to me like somebody's just not trying.

> *The lights rise stage left:*

BELLE: Don't worry, Ally, one day the right fella will come along for you.

ALLY: See, I don't know if I believe that anymore. I mean, it doesn't happen for every girl.

BELLE: Well, no, not for the wicked or the unattractive. But you have to believe! I'm proof it can all work out. I just know that one day a special guy is going to brutally imprison your father and take you as a hostage in exchange and after verbally abusing you, you'll fall madly in love! And as soon as he changes everything about himself physically, you can marry and live happily ever after in his secluded home with nothing but his paid servants to keep you company! It's every Disney princess' dream!

ALLY: Actually, Belle wasn't a princess—

> *BELLE stomps on her foot, never dropping her smile.*

OW!

> *SUPERMAN is instructing MARK.*

SUPERMAN: All right, Mark, write down everything I say for your personal ad. You can't lose with this one.

> *SUPERMAN does leg squats as he thinks. MARK writes everything down on a notepad.*

A KIND OF LOVE STORY

SUPERMAN (CONT'D): "One spectacular guy looking for a like-minded lady to share his Fortress of Solitude. If you're a kind, generous, loving, super woman, I'd like to be your super man— JK! But seriously... I can fly anywhere in the solar system, but only you can take me to heaven. P.S. No fatties." *(To Mark)* How's that sound?

MARK: I just don't know if this really reflects who I am.

SUPERMAN: Come on now, Mark, you're going to have to be willing to work a little harder.

ALLY: I've spent my whole life trying, maybe I should try... not trying.

BELLE: Ally, that sounds defeatist! I keep telling you—

SUPERMAN: I'll say it again—

BELLE & SUPERMAN: It's not that easy!

SUPERMAN and BELLE notice each other.

SUPERMAN: Hey.

BELLE: Hey.

SUPERMAN: You wanna...

BELLE: Yeah.

They exit together, with SUPERMAN preparing to take flight.

NARRATOR: Mark and Ally consoled themselves with the old belief that there was someone out there for everyone. And here's the universe's great secret: there is. But these two wouldn't meet today. In fact, no one could say when they would meet. Or if they would. Because here's the universe's other great secret: some people live their whole lives without ever actually meeting their soulmate. Mark and Ally might end up being two of those people.

The lights start to fade...

ALLY: Wait, what?

MARK: For real?

As we blackout:

MARK: Well, that sucks!

Blackout.

The music swells.

TITLE CARD – "A KIND OF LOVE STORY"

SCENE 2
TITLE CARD – "CHAPTER ONE: KISSING FROGS"

Melancholy music plays in the blackness. The lights rise on ALLY and MARK.

NARRATOR: Mark and Ally share more in common than a lifelong desire to be in love and the inability to find it. Both are the kind of friends you call when you're sick and need a chicken soup delivery. In fact, they'll probably make you some from scratch. Both strongly believe "Evil Dead 2" is a remake of the first one, not a sequel. And both have friends who are endless with helpful advice about relationships.

Mark's friend BOB and Ally's friend KELLY enter.

BOB: There's someone out there for everyone. Look, I was miserable for years before I met Diane!

MARK: You were 19!

BOB: Right? So it will happen for you! You just gotta hang in there!

KELLY: You just have to put yourself out there.

ALLY: But I do! I socialize, I'm active in arts and charitable causes, I've gone on blind dates and asked guys out and generally made myself completely available!

KELLY: Hm. You know, you always find the right person when you're not looking.

ALLY: Wait. Those are total contradictions! How can I put myself out there and not be looking at the same time?

KELLY is stuck. She tries to say something... then pushes ALLY down and runs away. BOB exits, too. As the NARRATOR speaks, MARK and Ally exit.

NARRATOR: Desperate times call for desperate measures from desperate people. For Ally, that meant she couldn't do something pathetic like spend another Saturday night with a gallon of ice cream and season 2 of "Sex and the City."

ALLY enters carrying ice cream and a DVD. As soon as she hears this, she exits.

Because that would just be sad. For Mark, that meant a date with a co-worker he didn't really think was right for him, but he wanted to keep an open mind. Lucy Andrews was the girl you told blonde jokes about. She wasn't ill-intentioned, but there wasn't a lot beneath the surface. Her favorite TV show is "NCIS: LA."

MARK sits at a table across from LUCY ANDREWS. Lucy is texting on her Blackberry and not even looking at Mark, who waits patiently. Finally, she puts it down.

LUCY: I'm having a great time.

MARK: So am I. It's nice to get to know people outside the station.

LUCY: Yeah, especially as the new girl.

MARK: I have to say, I'm impressed with how quickly you've moved up. I mean, from weathergirl to anchor in 90 days.

LUCY: I think it's kind of pathetic to be stuck in such a low-profile position for so long. It just shows how unvalued you are, don't you think?

MARK: I suppose.

LUCY: So. How long have you been a copywriter?

MARK: Six years.

LUCY: Oh.

MARK: I don't think I make much of an impression.

LUCY: That's not true! I've heard great things about you!

MARK: Yeah?

LUCY: Sure! You know Douglas, the segment producer? He said you're completely overqualified to be researching.

MARK: Douglas said that?

LUCY: Yes! He said you're good enough to be a reporter, that you have the brains and the talent to be on camera. He said you'd be a big star if our society wasn't so obsessed with looks.

MARK: Ah.

LUCY: Wait. That was kind of an insult, wasn't it?

MARK: Little bit.

LUCY: Shit. I'm sorry. I really shouldn't speak on my own. That's why I admire what you writers do so much. You're so good with... with...

MARK: Words?

LUCY: Yeah, you choose your words very wisely. I read your copy on the presidential visit. It was really clever, and I'll tell you the truth, all that president stuff bores me to death.

MARK: Well, thank God he's not in the news much.

LUCY: Exactly.

MARK: Oh, see, that was sarcasm. I don't think you got the reference.

LUCY: No, no I get it. Thank you!

> *As their lights fade, lights rise stage left. There is a knock on the door. ALLY enters in a robe.*

ALLY: One second!

NARRATOR: Ally, for her part, had sunk even lower than Mark. Rather than a blind date or a Craigslist hook up, she had called upon the lowest of life forms to help ease her loneliness: the ex-boyfriend.

> *She opens the door, revealing MAX BROCKMAN, leaning against the door frame, chewing gum loudly.*

NARRATOR (CONT'D): Max Brockman could be charming and charismatic when it served him to be. The rest of the time, he was an unapologetic narcissist who thought that just because he was upfront about his personality defects, that made his behavior acceptable. His favorite movie is "Precious." He finds it hilarious.

ALLY: Hey there.

MAX: Heyyyyy.

ALLY: Come on in.

> *He saunters in. She steps back to the couch. An awkward pause.*

Hey, did you happen to read my column today? I mentioned that marina we visited down south.

MAX: Nah. You still doing that writing thing?

ALLY: Yeah. So... do you like my hair?

MAX: Why? You cut it?

ALLY: I used to be a brunette.

MAX: Really? You sure?

> *They stand, facing each other, silently.*

So... you going to come over or you want me to do my thing from here?

> *She smiles weakly, makes her way over to him. They begin to kiss deeply. Suddenly, ALLY begins coughing uncontrollably. MAX slaps her on the back a couple times. Ally coughs up his gum into her hand.*

ALLY: I think this is yours.

MAX: Oh. Thanks, babe.

> *He pops it back in his mouth and starts to kiss her again. As the lights rise stage right, MARK is in the midst of an emotional story. LUCY looks bored.*

MARK: But I loved my mother more than anything. Now it's just me and my sister, who reminds me so much of her. And I'll never forget, just before she died, she gave me this one piece of advice that I've lived by all my life—

> *LUCY's cell phone goes off. (It plays something ridiculous and inappropriate.)*

LUCY: Oh, my phone! One sec.

> *She answers.*

Go for Lucy. Hey, what's up? No, I'm not doing anything. Yeah? Yeah?

> *She laughs uncontrollably.*

A KIND OF LOVE STORY

LUCY (CONT'D): That sounds great. I'll be there. Just finishing up a date.

She looks at MARK.

I don't know. A four. Maybe a five on a slow night. Brown hair, googly eyes. You know, he's a NICE GUY. Okay, see you then. Bye!

She hangs up the phone.

Sorry about that, important call.

MARK: Oh, was it work?

LUCY: No, just this guy I'm seeing.

MARK: A guy you're seeing?

LUCY: Yeah.

MARK: Like... dating?

LUCY: Uh-huh.

Beat.

Oh, I get it. You're going to get all jacked up because I'm seeing someone other than you tonight.

MARK: Tonight? Wait—

LUCY: Sure, he's my 9 o'clock. You thought this was like an exclusive thing, huh? I get this all the time with guys, they fall in love with me way too fast. It's a curse.

MARK: No, no, that's not it, it's just... look, why did you agree to dinner with me if you're seeing someone else tonight?

LUCY: A girl's gotta eat.

MARK: This isn't going well, is it?

LUCY: What's that?

MARK: This whole thing. I don't think you like me very much.

LUCY: I like you fine.

MARK: Really?

LUCY: No. Look, it's nothing personal. I'll see this date thing through and all. I'll even let you cop a feel when I hug you at the end. You're just not my type. I like classy guys who order wine and eat foie gras. You drink beer and eat pizza. Hey, you know what? You're more like my roommate. She reads books and things. I should introduce you to her— you two would hit it off. One woman's trash is another's treasure and all. You want her number?

MARK: Uh... no, that's cool.

LUCY: Whatever. Just trying to help.

Her phone rings.

Oh, it's my 11 o'clock. Be right back.

She exits as the lights fade on them and stage left. ALLY is sitting on the couch as MAX gets dressed.

ALLY: Oh, are you heading out already?

MAX: Yeah. Why, you got another round in you?

ALLY: No— I just... thought maybe we could talk. I mean, what's going on in your world?

MAX: What are we, girlfriends? What's with all the chatter?

ALLY: I guess I just miss talking to you. We used to have some great conversations. Now it's just all about sex.

MAX: I know. Isn't it great?

ALLY: I mean... do you miss me at all?

MAX: What do you mean? You're right here.

ALLY: Don't you get that I'm crazy about you? That I always have been. Don't you understand that when you come here and tell me you don't want my love or even my friendship, what that does to me?

MAX: Whoa, Ally. You knew we had a deal. I mean, if you want to go changing the rules, we can just forget this whole thing. Is that what you want? You want me to go and never come back?

ALLY looks torn.

NARRATOR: If this were a movie, this would be the point where the heroine embraced her own self-worth, where she finally told the asshole ex who never appreciated her that she was done for good. That being alone was better than being with him. But this was not a movie.

ALLY: No... it's cool.

MAX: All right. Hey, chin up, kiddo. You're still my back-up plan.

He winks and exits as the lights fade on ALLY. As the lights rise stage right, MARK is still alone at his table. He checks his watch. Sighs. The lights rise stage left. Ally is on the couch, watching TV, wearing a Snuggie. LUCY enters.

LUCY: Hey, roomie! What's up?

ALLY: Hey, Lucy. How was your dinner date?

LUCY: Dinner? Oh, crap, I totally forgot to say goodnight! Oh well, I'm sure he figured it out. Anyway, he was a nice guy, but you know the nice guys are all losers, right?

ALLY: Yeah. No, I don't.

LUCY: Exactly! Night, Ally!

ALLY: Good night.

NARRATOR: Ally and Mark were used to ending up alone on Saturday nights. But they each had a tradition they could count on.

She turns on the TV. As the lights rise stage right to full, MARK also enters in a Snuggie and turns on his TV. The "Star Wars" theme plays on both. They both begin to eat pizza and conduct along to the theme music.

NARRATOR (CONT'D): That night, Ally and Mark both went to bed with the same thought: that they had to believe. Believe that there was someone out there for them that was right, despite all evidence to the contrary. They didn't know who that person was, or why it was taking so long to find them, but they believed in that person. And whoever that person was, they would believe in them, too.

Blackout.

SCENE 3

TITLE CARD – "CHAPTER TWO: PLUGGING IN"

Melancholy music plays in the blackness. The lights rise on MARK and ALLY.

NARRATOR: Mark and Ally are born romantics struggling to stay that way in a world that often values appearance over substance. Both agree that Graham Chapman is the most underrated member of Monty Python. Both like to root for the underdog, so they registered Libertarian. And both grew up without the best parental supervision.

The parents enter: MARK'S DAD in a sports jersey with a beer, ALLY'S MOM a perfect 1950s-style housewife.

MARK'S DAD: Son, there is no such thing as limits. You can be anything you want to be. *(Beat)* Except gay. You're not gay, are you?

MARK: Dad, I tell you every day, no! I like girls!

MARK'S DAD: Are you sure? Because you used to wear that pink shirt—

MARK: I was five!

MARK'S DAD: Okay, okay. Just know I'm always here for you. And you can tell me anything. *(Knowingly)* Anything.

MARK: I'm not gay, Dad.

MARK'S DAD: That's cool, that's cool! Go team!

He goes to put his arm around him, but thinks better of it and punches his shoulder instead.

ALLY'S MOM: Now remember, honey, only order a salad on your date. Entrées are for married ladies. And if you go home hungry, don't worry. It's okay to be a little anorexic!

ALLY: But Mom, shouldn't I just be myself?

ALLY'S MOM laughs loud and long.

ALLY'S MOM: Oh, dear... no.

ALLY: You know, Mom, that's terrible advice. Generations of women battled for equal rights so that they could be recognized as being just as worthy as men. And furthermore—

Smiling tightly, her MOM pushes her down. EVERYONE exits.

NARRATOR: Ally would be the first person to admit she was a bit stuck in the past. She still watched movies on VHS. She was a journalist for a print magazine. And she had never tried internet dating. Fortunately, her shallow roommate Lucy was an expert.

LUCY and ALLY enter their apartment and look at the computer.

A KIND OF LOVE STORY

LUCY: 'Kay, stay away from loser sites like Plenty of Fish, they have no standards. And what is up with JDate? I couldn't find a single Christian. Stick with TheHunt4U.com. You can search not just by location and age, but sort it by hair color, eye color, even height!

ALLY: Wow. That's... thorough.

LUCY: If you know what you want, why not be specific and save everyone the trouble?

ALLY: Maybe that's the problem. All I want is a nice guy. Beyond that, I'm not entirely sure what I want.

LUCY: Well, what you don't want is to spend another weekend alone with your only human contact being the pizza delivery guy.

ALLY: Hey, Terry's cool. And I'm not totally alone. I've been spending time with Max...

> *LUCY groans, loud and long. Her groans grow increasingly dramatic.*

LUCY: He is such a douchebag!

ALLY: No, it's different this time!

> *LUCY groans.*

I'm not emotionally involved at all!

> *GROAN.*

And he's being really nice. For him. Look, he just sent me a text! Listen—

> *She opens her phone. MAX appears in a spotlight, texting.*

MAX: I'm bored. Text me a photo of your pussy.

> *ALLY snaps her phone shut as the lights go out on MAX.*

ALLY: Never mind.

LUCY: Now be very specific in your profile and only read other profiles with pictures and salaries listed as six figures and above. You do this long enough, you learn to read the warning signs.

ALLY: Like what?

LUCY: Can't spell... hate their mother... love their mother... list their religion as "Jedi."

ALLY: I just feel like we're sucking all the romance out of it.

LUCY: No, we're narrowing down the pool so you can get to the romance quicker. I'm very upfront in my profile about what I want. Let me show you.

> *Types.*

Here I am. PartyGirl69.

ALLY: What, were PartyGirl 1 through 68 taken? *(Reading)* "Super-cute beach bunny looking for a mate. Maybe for a lifetime, maybe for just tonight, let's get together and figure it out from there. Looking for a rich, successful partner, looks should be above average with an athletic body— no couch potatoes. Don't bother writing if you don't have a full head of natural hair. Speaking of, the majority of your hair should be on your head, not your body, or you must be willing to wax—" Jesus, Lucy!

LUCY: I know, you think I'm a bitch. But I'm the bitch getting fifty e-mails a day! Holla! Oh, speaking of, I have to go meet this guy for coffee. He's got potential, but I suspect there might be a little Photoshop at work in his pictures. That's another thing to look out for, make sure you get full body shots and that they're recent. Tell them to hold up today's paper and take a picture.

ALLY: He's not a hostage!

LUCY: Oh, and never, never make the first move. They have to write you. Have fun!

> *LUCY exits. ALLY ponders the screen before typing.*

ALLY: "Screen name... InfiniteJester. About me? I'm just looking for someone who makes me laugh. How you look is not at all important, I am more interested in your personality, your ambitions and your hobbies. Of course, a passion for The Kids in the Hall is a giant plus..."

> *As the lights fade on ALLY, MARK and BOB enter; Mark sits at his computer while Bob looks over his shoulder.*

NARRATOR: Mark himself had a little more experience with the Internet. He had been on TheHunt4U.com for six weeks under the alias Mr. MacGuffin. In that time, he had received one response to his personal ad. She was a hipster multimedia artist named Juneau Alaska.

> *JUNEAU enters, in a funky wool hat, thick glasses and whimsical clothing. Emo music plays in the background.*

He had hesitated meeting her after looking up her work online. She had attained some success for her YouTube video: "Embracing Loneliness." Clunky Glasses Magazine gave it four cappuccinos.

> *JUNEAU speaks with a non-descript, twee accent as she strikes various odd poses:*

JUNEAU: If you suddenly find yourself alone, be cool. It's all right to be alone. You can head to the 7-11 and talk to the clerk. Take a penny, leave two. He'll like that. Or call up a friend, just to chat. You'll see you can share being alone. Treat yourself to a movie and invite your coworkers. Soon, you'll be okay with being alone.

NARRATOR: Her other videos offered similar life philosophies.

JUNEAU: Remember that swimming is just bicycling... without the gravity. Talk is cheap because supply exceeds demand. When all you have is a hammer, everything looks like a nail.

BOB is entranced.

BOB: Wow. She's so profound.

MARK: What are you talking about? She's just babbling nonsense. And listen to this email.

As he opens an email, it makes a PING! sound.

JUNEAU: "Hey Mr. MacGuffin, nice play on McMuffin. Let's go to McDonald's sometime, but only ironically."

MARK: She doesn't even get that my screen name is an Alfred Hitchcock reference!

BOB: It is?

MARK: Yes! It's what he called the plot element that nobody really cares what it is, so long as it furthers the story! The MacGuffin!

BOB: Dude, if you expect someone to know that, the only person you're going to end up dating is Leonard Maltin. And I hear he's into some weird shit. So why don't you relax and just meet her?

NARRATOR: Mark knew his friend was right, and at last agreed to meet Juneau the following night. Ally, for her part, wasn't having much luck with the site. Though Lucy was regaling her with stories of all of her adventures, assuring her there were wild times to be had.

The lights rise as LUCY is gesticulating crassly as she tells a story. As the narration ends, a traumatized ALLY cuts her off.

ALLY: Well, I'm glad you've been enjoying yourself.

LUCY: Yeah, you just gotta be careful. Guys can really misrepresent themselves. This one guy seemed totally cool on the page and he picked me up in fucking Volkswagen. I mean...

She has no words.

So what about you? Met anyone promising yet?

ALLY: Oh here, let me show you.

She opens her computer.

In the last three days, I've gotten twenty e-mails. They all pretty much look like this.

She hits a key— a PING! sound. LUCY looks at the screen.

LUCY: That's a penis.

ALLY: I know. Who knew guys were more willing to show me their junk than their face?

Ping!

ALLY (CONT'D): Cock shot.

>*Ping!*

Cock shot.

>*Ping!*

Tasteful, black and white cock shot.

>*Ping!*

Look at the wide array of photos I have!

>*She goes through three more, each with a PING! LUCY and ALLY both turn their heads with each PING! On the last one, they turn simultaneously at a 90-degree angle.*

LUCY: Hey, I know him!

ALLY: Every time I go to open a new e-mail, I'm greeted by a cock. I've seen more wang than a Moyle this week. Why are guys so anxious to show off their junk?

LUCY: One of life's great mysteries. But you can't just give up. It's a numbers game. The next penis could be the one.

ALLY: I just... I don't know that I believe in the one perfect person for someone anymore.

>*A beat. A PING! sound.*

LUCY: Hey you got a message. That could be the right guy now. Take a look.

>*ALLY goes to open the e-mail. They both scream in dismay. Lights out stage left as they rise stage right on MARK, meeting JUNEAU at a coffee shop.*

NARRATOR: Mark's date with Juneau didn't start off promising. First of all, it turned out her name was spelled like Juneau the city, but actually pronounced "Gen-wa." Mark kept his expectations where they had begun—low. But a funny thing happened after a couple overpriced coffees. Mark began to see that Juneau was actually a very thoughtful person.

JUNEAU: I know the coffee isn't the best here, but it's privately owned and I want to help them out.

NARRATOR: They felt passionately about the same causes.

JUNEAU *(pounds table)*: And I swear, if Tatiana Maslany doesn't get an Emmy nomination this year for "Orphan Black," I will riot! *(Beat)* Also, I'm pro-choice.

NARRATOR: And she had a sense of humor.

JUNEAU: I don't eat fish because they're beautiful sea creatures. And roosters are noble birds. Basically, I won't eat anything with a face. Unless it's an ugly face. *(Beat; she starts laughing)* I'm just screwing with you, Mark, I eat like three burgers a day!

A KIND OF LOVE STORY

NARRATOR: Mark was having such a good time that he probably should have seen the inevitable coming at the end of the night.

As they get up to leave:

JUNEAU: Thanks for meeting me, Mark. I had a nice time.

MARK: It was nice. Next time we should take it up a level and grab dinner.

JUNEAU: Yeah... The thing is... I have a really busy career right now...

NARRATOR: Mark knew what was coming next. He knew it all too well.

JUNEAU: I just need to—

MARK: Take some time to figure out who you really are?

JUNEAU: Right. But I really hope—

MARK: We can be friends?

JUNEAU: Totally. You're such a nice guy, Mark. I'd love to be friends. Is that cool?

NARRATOR: There comes a day where every nice guy, even the nicest, has his breaking point. When he wants to ask where niceness is getting him after all these years, while the cruel and aloof seem to prosper. A day when he wants to stop masking his disappointment and give his honest reaction. Which would be...

The lights go red; MARK lets out a primal, furious scream. He knocks his chair over, runs out of the room and comes back in, tries to lift the table but can't, so he kicks it.

MARK *(with each kick)*: I... WASN'T... EVEN... INTERESTED... IN... YOU!! WHY... DOES... THIS... KEEP... HAPPENING????

He rips off her glasses and stomps up and down on them. After a beat, he composes himself and puts them back on her face.

NARRATOR: But this was not that day.

The lights shift back to normal.

MARK: Of course it's cool. Don't worry about it.

JUNEAU: Thanks, Mark. You know, whoever ends up with you is a lucky girl.

She pats his head and exits. MARK sighs and heads home.

NARRATOR: That night, Mark and Ally both thought about taking chances. How it hadn't always paid off for them, how their hearts should be nothing but scar tissue at this point, and yet they kept on trying.

ALLY sits at her computer, typing. MARK arrives home and stares at his screen, thinking. The lights begin to fade.

For Ally, taking a chance meant breaking Lucy's rules and writing a guy who had all the warning signs she'd been told to look out for: no photo, an unlisted income; just a profile that made her smile.

NARRATOR (CONT'D): For Mark, that meant not deleting that account that had only resulted in one depressing date in six weeks. They could both hold out a little longer. Because whoever was out there... was worth it.

> *As MARK goes to shut his computer, there is a PING! The lights rise back up a bit. He opens it and reads.*

ALLY: Hey, there. Love your screen name. I'm a huge Hitchcock fan.

> *MARK smiles and begins to type as we fade to blackout.*

SCENE 4

TITLE CARD – "CHAPTER THREE: VIRTUAL STRANGERS"

Melancholy music plays in the blackness. The lights rise on MARK and ALLY.

NARRATOR: Mark and Ally both have unconditional love to give, but no one worthy to bestow it upon. They're both the friends you call when you need a ride to the airport. They both secretly wonder if the Scientologists are right. And both often feel alone when surrounded by other people.

The friends enter: on Mark's side, it's JOHN and TAMMY, and BOB and DIANE. They are madly in love, even dressed alike, and chatting in a circle with MARK. On Ally's side are LUCY, LAUREN, and BRENDA.

TAMMY: I just love Mexican food! I could eat it for every meal!

MARK: You need to try LaQuinta, they make the best pico de gallo!

JOHN: What a great idea! Bob, let's take the ladies next week!

DIANE: Definitely! Let's do a couples night!

BOB: Speaking of, I have four extra tickets to the Philharmonic! You guys should join us!

DIANE: But that still leaves two tickets— hmmm. Do you know any other couples we could invite?

JOHN: Of course! Everyone's a couple!

They all laugh and clink glasses.

ALLY: The career is going really well. Things are good. I just... wish I could just find a nice guy.

LUCY: Oh my God, can you believe her? I keep telling her to up her standards. I mean, I won't go out with anyone who carries anything lower than a platinum card, am I right?

BRENDA: Lucy, you are just adorable! I need to set you up with my brother! You have to meet him!

LUCY: I don't know... does he have your nose?

LAUREN: No, you know who would be perfect for her? Tom! We should introduce her to Tom, he's a great guy! Are you free Friday?

LUCY: Well, I'm sort of into women this week, but I could make an exception. I have 4 p.m. Wednesday or 2 a.m. Thursday.

ALLY: I'm available Friday—

*LUCY looks at her, annoyed, and pushes her down.
EVERYONE exits as ALLY goes to her apartment.*

NARRATOR: Mark and Ally had enjoyed exchanging emails and found they had an easy rapport. But they were hesitant to take the final step and meet.

NARRATOR (CONT'D): Mark had been burned on his only Internet date, and Ally had some unresolved issues. The main one being her ex-boyfriend, Max Brockman.

MAX enters, getting dressed.

MAX: Heyyyyyy. You tricked me. It's my brother's last night in town and you lured me over here and now I'm late to meet him.

ALLY: How did I lure you? You called me.

MAX *(duh)*: You answered. I'm onto your little mind games, Ally, don't play innocent.

ALLY: Max... don't you ever want more than just sex? Don't you want someone you can turn to when things are bad? Don't you want that one person who loves and adores you above all others?

MAX: Nope.

He notes her reaction and groans.

Okay, what's this about?

ALLY: It's stupid. I was watching this movie the other day and I know it's not real life, but it really got to me—

MAX: Oh God, let me guess: "Sleepless in Seattle?" "When Harry Met Sally?" You know Meg Ryan can't keep a man in real life! Fuck Hollywood and their stupid ideals of romance for ruining things for nice guys like me!

ALLY: No! It was... "Armageddon." And it's terrible, I know it is, but there's this astronaut played by Will Patton and he's separated from his wife and kid and she doesn't know he's going into space to try and blow up this asteroid and save the earth. But when he's up there, facing death, all he can do is think about her, and how he has to do this to save the people he loves, even though they will never know his sacrifice. And then when the plan goes wrong and she sees him on TV and realizes he's in danger— it's like all their problems, all their differences, fall away in that moment and all she cares about is that he makes it home safe. And I know it's stupid, cheesy, over-directed movie that has a love song by Steven Tyler that plays while his daughter is having sex onscreen and that's just creepy, but I just started crying. Because when he comes back and they see each other on the tarmac— and I have no idea how she got there, apparently NASA has really shitty security or something— all I could think was how much I wanted what they had— I wanted to be the man on a mission whose life was given a purpose by this other person. Or the woman whose love could inspire a man to save the world. I wanted someone to come home to. Who would look for me in a room before all others. And I thought that could be you.

After a beat:

MAX: Geez... spoiler alert much? I guess I can delete "Armageddon" off the DVR.

A KIND OF LOVE STORY

ALLY: You're never going to magically wake up one day and see my worth, are you?

MAX: Ally, that's not what I'm looking for. But you know I care about you. Look I even got this for you.

He hands her a card.

ALLY: This is a coupon to a waxing studio.

MAX: That's right. I like a clean plate. See you next time! *(Popping back in)* Oh and— you're welcome!

He shoots her fingerguns and exits.

NARRATOR: Ally knew in her logical mind that Max wasn't ever going to be the man she wanted. And right then, she needed someone to talk to who understood where she was coming from. Fortunately, she had an appointment that night with just such a person.

MARK is already at his computer as ALLY sits at hers. They speak conversationally as they type.

ALLY: Hey there.

MARK: Hey! There you are! Sorry, I'm new to this whole chat feature. It's nice to "meet" you.

ALLY: Nice to meet you. I've really enjoyed emailing.

MARK: It's so rare to find someone who equally appreciates "Cinema Paradiso" and "Re-Animator".

ALLY: Sure. I actually think "Cinema Paradiso" could have been improved by adding a few decapitations.

MARK: LOL. Agreed.

ALLY *(yelling)*: I LOVE THE "RE-ANIMATOR MOVIES"! Oops, sorry. Caps lock.

MARK: We should have a marathon. When we meet IRL.

ALLY: IRL?

MARK: In Real Life. Sorry, I forget you hate those abbreviations.

ALLY: I don't hate them, I'm just afraid I'm using them wrong. I thought I was saying Good For You and learned I'd just told someone to go fuck themselves. Plus, I never believing anyone when they tell me they're LOL-ing. I always want to say "Really? REALLY?"

MARK: That's why I use LLOL, for "Literally Laughing Out Loud." So they know I mean it.

ALLY: I prefer LLOLPWIJPL. "Literally Laughing Out Loud to the Point Where I Just Peed a Little."

MARK *(laughing)*: OMG. LLOL. Sincerely. Look, I didn't mean to be presumptuous earlier. If you're not ready to meet, it's okay.

ALLY: I really like talking to you, MacGuffin. I'm just a little gun shy. In the past year I've been out with three commitment-phobes, one mama's boy and a guy who believes the flu shots were designed by the government to make us crave beets.

MARK: I understand, believe me. I just... have a good feeling about you, InfiniteJester. I know that sounds ridiculous, I don't even know your real name.

ALLY: It's not ridiculous, it's an adventure. It could be like that scene in "You've Got Mail" where Meg Ryan agrees to meet Tom Hanks at this little cafe. They don't know what each other looks like or even their names... but she has her copy of "Pride and Prejudice."

MARK: But we would never do something so cheesy.

ALLY: Of course not.

MARK: It would have to be—

ALLY: We'd do—

MARK & ALLY: "Pride and Prejudice and Zombies"!

ALLY: OMG!

MARK: LOL!

ALLY: I admit it, I find it silly but romantic. Truth is, I'm kind of a sap.

MARK: I understand. Hey, don't tell anyone, but I'm the guy who always cries at "Armageddon." *(Beat)* You still there? Oh God, I lost you on that one, didn't I?

ALLY: No. Actually, I think we should meet. Are you free tomorrow?

NARRATOR: And so the plan was made. The two strangers would meet at a little hideaway Ally suggested, both carrying copies of "Pride and Prejudice and Zombies." For the first time in a long while, Mark and Ally believed they were doing everything right.

As MARK sits at the cafe, LUCY enters to yell at ALLY.

LUCY: You are doing everything wrong! You don't have his name, you don't know what he looks like! He could be a serial killer! Or disfigured! Or an actor!

ALLY: I'm not like you, Lucy. None of that matters to me.

LUCY: You are making a huge mistake.

There is a knock at the door. LUCY goes to answer it.

ALLY: I don't care! What have I got to lose? Really— what's stopping me?

LUCY enters with MAX, who is out of sorts.

LUCY: Hey, did somebody order a douchebag delivery?

ALLY: Max?

MAX: Hey, Ally. I need to talk to you.

A KIND OF LOVE STORY 23

ALLY: You want to talk? You?

MAX: Look, I've been thinking a lot about what you said. And last night, I Netflixed "Armageddon." And you were right. I would totally risk my life blowing up an asteroid for Liv Tyler.

ALLY: That's actually not the point—

MAX: I don't want to go into space and have no one to come back to. I want someone waiting who totally gets me and realizes how awesome I am. That's you, Ally. So let's do it, let's try having a real r-r-r... *(He can't say the word)* R-r-r-...relationship! Whoa.

ALLY: Max, I have to be somewhere—

MAX: Can't you see what I'm going through here? We need to talk about our feelings and shit. You can't abandon me now!

ALLY is torn. MAX gives her pleading eyes.

ALLY: Lucy... I need you to do something for me. Please. Go to the Laurent Cafe and find Mr. MacGuffin. He'll have a copy of "Pride and Prejudice and Zombies" on him. Please tell him I'm sorry and something came up, but I'll explain later.

LUCY: Ugh. Okay, but only because it's next to the pharmacy and I have to pick up my Valtrex anyway. Plus he's going to be vulnerable after being stood up!

ALLY: You're a good friend.

As LUCY exits:

LUCY: I know, right?

MAX: Ally, hold me. *(Choking up)* It was so beautiful... I couldn't believe Bruce Willis wouldn't get off the asteroid...

NARRATOR: Ally could have never predicted this was how her night would end up. And she had no way of knowing that the woman she sent to let her date down gently... would have once dated him herself.

LUCY enters the restaurant. She looks around, then spots MARK.

LUCY: Hey! Don't I work with you? It's Matt, right?

MARK: It's Mark, actually.

LUCY: No, I'm pretty sure it's Matt. What are you doing here, it's so far from the office. People only come here when they're embarrassed to be seen with someone!

MARK: Actually, Lucy, I sort of want to be alone right now—

LUCY *(sitting down)*: I hear you. I would never set foot in this dive except I'm doing a favor for my roommate. She needs me to blow off some loser she had a blind date with cuz right now she's getting it from her ex-boyfriend.

MARK: Ah.

LUCY: She can't make dinner cuz her appetite is being satisfied, if you know what I mean.

MARK: I think I get it.

LUCY: And I'm not talking about food, you know!

MARK: No, that's apparent—

LUCY: She's having sex!

MARK: Ah, thanks for clearing that up.

LUCY: Anyway, joke's on her cuz I don't see any single, straight guys here so I guess she got stood up. I don't think she'll take it too hard, though. Since she's taking it hard right now, if you know what I mean! I mean—

MARK: Got it! Thank you!

LUCY grabs his book.

LUCY: Hey, whatcha reading? Any good?

MARK: You wouldn't like it, it's... non-fiction.

LUCY makes a disgusted noise and throws the book back to MARK. She gets up and leaves.

Good night, Lucy.

MARK heads home as the lights rise on ALLY on the couch, MAX's head in her lap, sleeping.

NARRATOR: Mark wasn't going to allow himself too be too disappointed, as there was no point in it. He was the kind of guy who was used to not getting what he wanted. So he would chalk it up to another lesson learned... online dating was not for him.

MARK opens his computer and begins to type. ALLY strokes MAX's hair.

MARK: Account... deleted.

MAX: Ally, I've been meaning to ask... have you put on weight?

ALLY sighs.

NARRATOR: What Mark didn't yet know... and what Ally was only starting to realize... is that sometimes the worst thing that can happen... is getting what you wanted.

Blackout.

SCENE 5

TITLE CARD – "CHAPTER FOUR: SINGULAR COUPLES"

Melancholy music plays in the blackness. The lights rise on MARK and ALLY.

NARRATOR: Mark and Ally both wonder if they're ever going to find someone who loves them just the way they are. Both secretly hope that their toys really do come to life when they're not looking. And both have friends who epitomize their idea of a perfect couple.

On Mark's side, BOB and DIANE enter. On Ally's, it's SAM and BRENDA.

For Mark, his ideal couple is Bob and Diane, who met each other their first day of college and have never spent a day apart. They make great partners at charades.

Bob starts making gestures.

MARK: Two words!! Oh, a book!

DIANE: The Koran!

BOB: YES!

They squeal and kiss.

NARRATOR: They understood each other's needs.

DIANE: Honey, what were you thinking for dinner tonight?

BOB: I don't know, maybe a lightly braised lamb shank with pureed potatoes garnished with blue cheese and pecans on the side and a spinach salad tossed in a white vinaigrette.

DIANE: Oh, that's going to be a problem... cuz they only had red vinaigrette!!!

She holds out a plate. They squeal again.

NARRATOR: It was like they had a sixth sense about each other.

As he starts to eat his meal, DIANE hands him a Band-Aid.

BOB: A Band-Aid? What for—

As he's slicing his meat, he cuts himself. With an "Ooh!" he grabs his finger, realizes he has the Band-Aid, and lovingly kisses her.

NARRATOR: For Ally, her perfect couple came in the form of her friend Brenda, who was madly in love with her boyfriend, Sam.

SAM is planting kisses on BRENDA's neck and shoulder as she speaks.

BRENDA: If you've never been to Italy, you must visit the Amalfi Coast. We have a home there, you're welcome to stay.

ALLY: That sounds amazing!

SAM: Yes, yes, the more the merrier!

BRENDA: Oh Ally, we so enjoy your company. We really like you a lot!

ALLY: Thank you so much!

SAM: What about you... do you like us?

ALLY: Well, of course! You're both always so nice to me!

BRENDA: So you... really like us? Because we really... really... like you.

They flank her on either side.

ALLY: Oh, wow, I can't believe this is happening... again. I'm sorry guys, I'm super flattered, but I'm just not interested. You understand, right? We can still be friends? ...Italy?

SAM pushes ALLY into BRENDA, who pushes her down. EVERYONE exits.

NARRATOR: Though neither was an expert on relationships, Ally was trying her hand at one. Unfortunately, she and Max had already settled into a comfortable routine.

The lights rise on ALLY in her apartment. MAX walks in, unzips his pants, sits on the couch and picks up the remote.

MAX: Beer me.

ALLY hands him a beer.

NARRATOR: Ally even tried to get him to broaden his horizons by buying him educational presents.

She gives MAX a book.

MAX: A book? Is this some kind of joke?

ALLY: It's the new Casey Collins book. She's my favorite author.

MAX: I thought your favorite author was Stephanie Meyer.

ALLY: No, that's you.

MAX: Oh, right. Renesmee!

ALLY: I thought you could read it and we could talk about it. I have so many thoughts I want to share with someone.

MAX *(flipping through it)*: No pictures? Arughghghg...

ALLY: She's this amazing feminist author and she's coming to town later this month. I'm hoping I can get an interview. She writes about women becoming empowered through fairy tales.

MAX: Aughghgh! It just gets worse and worse!

ALLY looks disgusted.

NARRATOR: Ally found herself needing a break, so she planned a girls' night in. It would be a good opportunity to spend some quality time with her friends... and get away from Max.

MAX: So what do you do on these girls' nights, anyway? Are you gonna kiss?

ALLY: Just hang out. Drink. Talk. It's just me and Lucy and Kelly.

MAX: Kelly? She hates me.

ALLY: No, she doesn't. She actually invited us to come up to Napa at the end of the month, you know.

MAX: We can't, we have plans that weekend. My neighbor is having an anniversary party and we're going.

ALLY: We are?

MAX: Yeah. Isn't the whole point of being in a relationship that you have someone to drag to these stupid parties? I'm so glad that person is you, Ally.

ALLY: You are?

MAX: Hell, yes! You are so much hotter than my friends' girlfriends! Winning! *(Off her look)* Oh great, what now?

ALLY: Max, see, when you say things like that, it makes me feel like you don't have any interest in me as a person. It's treating me like an object or a prize. *(Sigh)* You don't understand, do you?

MAX: No, no, I totally understand. Clearly, you're about to start your period. I'll see you in three days. Hm, better make it four, just to play it safe.

He starts to exit, only to be cut off by LUCY and KELLY entering.

LUCY: Hey, look who I found wandering the hallway! Thought I'd take her in out of pity.

KELLY: Hey I know its girls only but I figured you'd be okay if I brought my friend Chuck!

She produces a bottle of wine.

NARRATOR: Kelly Colson was Ally's oldest and dearest friend. They met the first day of high school, when they bumped into each other, dropped their Heroes Trapper Keepers, and found out they were both Team Sylar. Kelly is also the only woman who terrifies Max Brockman.

MAX: Hey, Kelly. How are you?

KELLY: You again? Ugh. *(To Ally)* How's my favorite blonde gnome?

ALLY: Hi Kelly!

They go to hug.

I'll talk to you later Max.

She senses him hesitating.

We're not going to kiss!

MAX: Cool. Later.

He can't wait to leave.

KELLY: All right, what kind of host are you? I've been here 30 seconds and I have yet to get my drink on.

ALLY: Sorry, sorry!

As LUCY starts to exit:

Lucy, where are you going? Aren't you staying with us?

LUCY: Oh, about that. I'm totally down for the whole rah-rah sisterhood female empowerment thing, just not tonight. I gots me a non-committal hookup. Later, bitches!

She exits.

KELLY: Wow, she's really grown as a person.

The lights rise on BOB and MARK at a bar.

NARRATOR: Mark, for his part, was also spending some quality time with his friend Bob. After being burned on his last few experiences with women, he was looking forward to a guys' night out.

BOB: Are you trying? I mean, really trying? What happened to that girl you were chatting up online?

MARK: It didn't work out.

BOB: What are you looking for?

MARK: You know... someone who gets me. Who isn't always on the lookout for the bigger, better deal but sees me for what I really am... and likes it. Is that too much to ask? I guess we can't all have what you and Diane have.

BOB: Yeah. I'm thinking of cheating on her.

MARK: What? What happened?

BOB: Nothing. She's great. I adore her. But we met so young, and ten years is a long time to be with one person.

MARK: Not if that person is Diane.

BOB: You always had a little thing for her. And I don't blame you, she's great. I just don't want to live the rest of my life wondering, you know? If I missed out.

MAX enters the bar, book in hand.

MARK: This doesn't sound like you. It sounds more like—

BOB *(spots Max)*: Max! Oh hey, you've got to meet this guy. Max, over here!

MAX approaches them.

MAX: Hey, Bob, what's going on? Where's the old ball and chain?

BOB: You know, behind the stove where she belongs.

They laugh.

(Sees Mark's reaction)

Kidding, kidding! Hey, this is my friend, Mark. Mark, my neighbor, Max.

MAX: Heyyyyyy.

MARK: Oh, you're reading Casey Collins' new book.

BOB: Mark here is a copywriter at WNCB. He's into books and stuff like that.

MAX: Ugh, sorry to hear it.

MARK: No, I'm Casey's biggest fan. In fact, she's—

MAX: Yeah? Here you go, knock yourself out. My girlfriend is trying to make me read it.

MAX throws the book at MARK.

MARK: Oh, well shouldn't you maybe take a look then?

MAX: Nah, that's what Wikipedia's for.

His phone rings.

One sec. Yeah? Yeah, spare key under the door. Just let yourself in.

He hangs up.

I gotta run. Booty calls!

BOB: Ooh, is it that cute blonde that's been coming around lately?

MAX: Bob, you know a gentleman never tells. Which is why I can say yes, yes it is.

They laugh and high five. MAX exits.

BOB: See that's exactly what I'm talking about. Max is out there, playing the field, having a great time. You would not believe the women that come in and out of his place. It's just so easy to find someone these days!

MARK says nothing as the lights fade. The lights rise on ALLY and KELLY on the couch, drinking.

NARRATOR: Two bottles of wine into the evening, Kelly confronted Ally on her relationship in that way only your oldest and dearest friend can.

KELLY: So, are you an idiot or just a masochist? I mean, seriously— Max again? Let me guess, you're going to tell me he's different now? That things have changed.

ALLY: No. He's still horrible. But I've seen the guy he can be and there were times when it was wonderful. Plus, this is what I said I wanted for so long, I feel like I have to try and make it work.

KELLY: But as long as Max is in your life being your meantime guy, you're never going to open yourself up to finding the lifetime guy. And I know that's what you really want.

ALLY: We don't always get what we want. And sometimes, it's enough.

KELLY: Not for you. You deserve the best. Come on, I know you. You're Ally O'Neill. You like pug dogs and conspiracy theories and some guy named Richard Jenkins. And the perfect guy is out there for you.

A long pause. Barely audibly:

ALLY: But what if he never finds me?

KELLY: Do you remember how long it took me to break up with that loser Reed? I was so scared that I would never meet anyone else. But I was wrong.

ALLY: You were 15!

KELLY: Look... at first I was afraid. I was petrified. Kept thinking I could never live without him by my side.

ALLY: What?

KELLY: But then I spent so many nights, thinking how he did me wrong.

ALLY: What are you doing?

KELLY *(singing now)*:
BUT I GREW STRONG! AND I LEARNED HOW TO GET ALONG!

ALLY: Gloria Gaynor? Really?

KELLY goes into full song mode.

KELLY:
GO ON NOW GO!
WALK OUT THE DOOR!
JUST TURN AROUND NOW,
'CAUSE YOU'RE NOT WELCOME ANYMORE.

Lucy enters, in the midst of shaving her legs for her big night, joining in:

KELLY & LUCY:
WEREN'T YOU THE ONE WHO TRIED TO HURT ME WITH GOODBYES
DID YOU THINK I'D CRUMBLE
DID YOU THINK I'D LAY DOWN AND DIE?
OH NO, NOT I
I WILL SURVIVE
OH AS LONG AS I KNOW HOW TO LOVE
I KNOW I'LL STAY ALIVE
I'VE GOT ALL MY LIFE TO LIVE
I'VE GOT ALL MY LOVE TO GIVE
AND I'LL SURVIVE
I WILL SURVIVE! HEY, HEY!

ALLY applauds in disbelief. They start up again:

I'VE GOT ALL MY LIFE TO LIVE
I'VE GOT ALL MY LOVE TO GIVE
AND I'LL SURVIVE
I WILL SURVIVE! HEY, HEY!

A KIND OF LOVE STORY

> *Lights fade and rise on: MARK and BOB, returning home. DIANE enters.*

DIANE: Hey guys, how was dinner?

BOB: Great honey, but I think I had—

DIANE: A little too much to drink? I was afraid of that. I put out some Tums and an ice pack next to your pajamas.

> *BOB starts to ask—*

—Yes, the flannel ones.

> *He starts to ask—*

—With the little coffee cups on them.

BOB: You're the best. G'night, Mark!

> *BOB exits as DIANE turns to MARK.*

DIANE: You doing okay, Mark? I mean, really? You know you don't have to pretend with me.

MARK: I'm fine, thank you, Diane. Look, I was a little disappointed I never even got to meet the girl but you know... onward and upward.

DIANE: It'll happen for you, Mark. Any girl would be lucky to have you. Just hang in there. You'll survive this.

MARK: Right.

DIANE: I mean it, Mark. Say it. Say, "I deserve the best. I will survive this. She is out there."

MARK: Diane, that's silly—

DIANE: Say it, Mark, you have to say it to believe it.

MARK: I just feel ridiculous—

> *DIANE grabs his arm and twists it behind him; MARK cries out in surprise.*

DIANE: Say it, Mark! Say it!

MARK: I deserve the best! I will survive! I will!

> *She releases him.*

DIANE: Just keep repeating that. Make it your mantra. I promise you, you'll find the right girl.

> *She kisses him on the cheek and exits.*

MARK: I don't think that's how "The Secret" works.

> *He walks home to his apartment as the lights rise on ALLY and KELLY passed out in her apartment.*

NARRATOR: That night, Mark and Ally asked themselves if they were foolish to hold out for what they believed in. Did their perfect match really exist and if so, why was it taking so long?

> *ALLY cuddles her wine bottle as MARK nurses a beer and flips through Casey's book. Both murmur:*

MARK & ALLY: "...I've got all my life to live... I've got all my love to give...and I'll survive... I will survive... hey hey..."

NARRATOR: For Ally, the decision couldn't have come a moment too soon. Because as much as we'd like to believe in change...

> *Lights rise on MAX, standing in his apartment. LUCY enters.*

MAX: Heyyyy.

LUCY: Hey. Here's your key.

> *She hands it to him. They kiss passionately.*

NARRATOR: ...some people never do.

> *Blackout.*
>
> *INTERMISSION.*

END OF ACT I

ACT II

SCENE 6
TITLE CARD – "CHAPTER FIVE: TO-DO LIST"

Melancholy music plays in the blackness.

NARRATOR: This is the story of two people who were made for each other. A man and a woman destined to fall madly in love. If only they could ever meet.

The lights rise as MARK and ALLY enter.

Mark and Ally are kind and loyal souls searching for love in a world that doesn't always value such qualities. Both have always wanted to make an omelet out of Cadbury crème eggs. Both will argue until they're hoarse that the end of "Inception" was not all a dream. And both have a long history of being terrible at flirting.

DIANE enters on Mark's side; DEAN and LUCY enter on Ally's side.

When Mark first met Diane in college at a Gloria Steinem book signing, he just tried too hard.

MARK: So, maybe we can see a movie sometime?

DIANE: That sounds like fun. Anything but the re-release of "Snow White."

MARK: Oh, I know, isn't Disney the worst? I mean, some guy stumbles on a dead woman in the forest and has to kiss her? That's not true love, that's necrophilia. Right? I mean, she could never live up to his fantasy. Typical Disney portrayal of women: beautiful, sought-after ciphers with no real life of their own. Am I right?

DIANE: I just meant that I already promised to take my niece to see it... since it's my favorite movie of all time.

MARK: Oh.

DIANE: You must think I'm so silly. A grown woman, watching fairy tales—

BOB enters, whistling.

MARK: Oh, there's my friend Bob. Bob, this is Diane.

BOB: Hey. I have a penis.

DIANE is charmed; they exit together.

NARRATOR: For Ally, flirting was tough enough without constantly being upstaged by her roommate, Lucy.

ALLY is trying to talk to DEAN.

ALLY: This is a really nice gallery, the art is gorgeous. I'm mostly a Salvador Dalí girl, but I'm really beginning to appreciate the McDonalds.

LUCY: Ohmygawd listen to you! *(Snooty voice)* "I'm really beginning to appreciate McDonalds." Come on! Like, the only McDonalds you appreciate is the one that has McNuggets and shakes, am I right?

> *LUCY goes to high five ALLY, who just looks uncomfortable. DEAN is sympathetic.*

DEAN: Were you able to check out the Disney exhibit at the Skirball? Just stunning.

LUCY: Ohmygawd, remember that time we went to Disneyland and you had really terrible explosive diarrhea and they called you up on stage at Cinderella-bration, and you wouldn't go up because you had, like, no bowel control? Remember how awful that was? Ally? Ally, do you remember?

DEAN: MOMA has a new earth exhibit, too. They brought the butterfly pavilion from New York.

LUCY: Ack, don't tell her that, she hates butterflies! She's terrified of them!

DEAN: Nothing to be ashamed of, we all have our little quirks.

LUCY: She doesn't even like my tattoo, it freaks her out. See, I have a tattoo of two butterflies by my belly button, let me show you...

> *LUCY pulls up her shirt, revealing a tattoo— and her bra. DEAN stares at her chest.*

Aren't they cute? Anyway, you guys have fun talking art and stuff, I'm gonna get drunk and irresponsible! Woo!

> *She exits. ALLY and DEAN look at each other awkwardly.*

ALLY: So, that Disney exhibit—

DEAN: Look, Ally...

> *He puts his hands on her shoulders... then pushes ALLY down and chases after Lucy.*

Lucy! Wait up!

> *Lights dim and rise on MARK, talking to BOB and DIANE.*

NARRATOR: Mark's luck hadn't improved in recent years. Currently, he was regaling Bob and Diane with the adventures of his latest blind date, a dental hygienist introduced to him by his cousin.

BOB: She was a dog, right? That always happens when you don't get a picture first.

MARK: No, much to my relief, she was very attractive and quite bright. And she told me she was relieved too, when she saw me.

DIANE: That's great!

MARK: Yeah. She was afraid I would be Jewish.

A KIND OF LOVE STORY

DIANE: What?

MARK: Oh, it's not that she hates the Jews, you see. She just feels they should know better. They have the ability to change who they are if they wanted to. Not like the blacks.

BOB: No!

DIANE: Oh, Mark I'm so sorry.

MARK: I guess I know why she loves her job so much... making teeth nice and white.

BOB: Tough break, dude. Hey honey, any of that strawberry shortcake you made left?

DIANE: Yes, I set it on the counter so it would be the perfect temperature by now.

BOB: You're the best. Isn't she the best?

He exits. DIANE regards MARK.

DIANE: Did you guys behave yourselves tonight?

MARK: Always.

She regards him suspiciously.

DIANE: Mark. Can we talk frankly?

MARK: Of course.

A moment of nervousness for MARK, before DIANE grabs a paper tablet.

DIANE: Here's what we need to do. We are going to make a list of everything you could ever possibly want in a girl and then we are going to find her, I promise you.

MARK: Oh, I don't know-

DIANE: Mark, what do I keep telling you? You have to believe it to make it happen. Come on, tell me about your perfect woman.

As she writes, she is oblivious to how MARK is looking at her.

MARK: She should be funny. You know, an appreciation for Monty Python is a must.

DIANE: Well, of course.

MARK: She should love animals. And kids. And be generous. The kind of person who rarely thinks of herself first, but is always looking out for others. She should laugh easy. The kind of laugh that lights up her entire face. You know, the sort of girl who makes you feel at home wherever you are. She's confident, but she also underestimates herself. I mean, she's attractive... but in such a way that... maybe she isn't even aware of just how beautiful she is. Like, if she could only see herself the way I see her, she almost wouldn't recognize herself. You can't not feel good when she's around.

DIANE: Oh, Mark. She sounds amazing.

MARK: Yeah.

> *DIANE hands MARK the list.*

Diane. I know I'm Bob's friend. But I'm your friend too, aren't I?

> *A beat.*

DIANE: Mark, if you have something to say, just say it.

MARK: I just... I think Bob is having some kind of a mid-mid-life crisis. I think he takes you for granted. I'm sorry, I know it's not my place.

DIANE: Mark. Do you think I don't see what you see? When you're with someone for a long time, things change. Is this the way I imagined my life turning out? Did I have hopes and dreams and aspirations that I've had to trade in for the life I do have?

MARK: If you're unhappy—

DIANE: It's not that at all. You just make certain compromises. Remember how I wanted to honeymoon in Paris? I'd always dreamed of visiting the Louvre and seeing the Eiffel Tower. But we couldn't afford it, so we went camping. And it didn't matter because we were together. And we saw the most beautiful sunsets. Yes, I would love to still get to Paris some day but I wouldn't change it for the world. It's just a different kind of beautiful.

NARRATOR: Far less beautiful was the relationship Ally had managed to find herself in with the terrible Max Brockman.

> *ALLY goes to rest her head on his shoulder. MAX smiles and puts his arm around her. Then starts to not-so-subtly push her head down into his lap. Ally pushes him away and goes to the other end of the couch. Max gets up and starts thinking.*

Max wasn't good at many things, but he was an expert at disappointing Ally. Yet somehow he sensed, in that way men do, that he was losing his grip on her. And so he decided, in that way that childish men do, that it was time to turn up the charm.

> *MAX approaches ALLY; his tone and demeanor are totally changed— he's being SWEET.*

MAX: Hey, girlfriend! I thought we could just stay in tonight and snuggle. Maybe watch a movie?

ALLY: Really? Uh... okay, there's some new films on Netflix. I'd love to watch "Nell"!

MAX *(annoyed)*: Ohhhh! *(He switches to happy)* OHHHHHH! *(Through gritted teeth)* That sounds wonderful! It's not at all cloying or pretentious, I won't be tempted to laugh at all. Isn't Jodie Foster an inspiration?

NARRATOR: He even tried showering her with gifts.

MAX: I know you enjoy reading... and stuff. So... here's a book!

He tosses her a book. ALLY opens it.

ALLY: "Tijuana Bibles: Cartoon Porn From The Underground"?

MAX: Yeah. You like cartoons. You're always going on about Disney and Cinderella and stuff.

ALLY: Those are fairy tales, Max, not pornographic comic strips! Oh, there's an inscription!

MAX: What? Wait—

ALLY: "For Max, who brings max-imum pleasure to me. Heather." Max, did you regift this?

A beat. MAX heads for the door.

MAX: Heyyyyy what's the cutest thing someone could get for you? Your very own puppy!

He reaches outside and comes back with a small dog.

ALLY: You got me a puppy?? Max, he's adorable! What a little dollface! Oh, did you name him already?

She goes to look at his tags.

MAX: What?

ALLY: Oh, his name is Petey! So cute! And if he's found, it says to return him to the O'Leary residence...? Max? Is this someone else's dog?

MAX stares at her. A beat. He runs out the door. ALLY sighs and stares at her dog— she pulls out her cell and begins to phone the owner. The lights rise to full, as MARK comes home, looking at his list.

NARRATOR: That night, Mark and Ally thought over their respective lists. Were they asking for too much, to find one person who met all their criteria? And if that person was out there— what if they were with the wrong person? Was it too late to find their happily ever after?

Blackout.

SCENE 7

TITLE CARD – "CHAPTER SIX: BRIEF ENCOUNTER"

The lights rise as MARK and ALLY enter.

NARRATOR: Mark and Ally both grew up believing in fairy tale romances, but have yet to find their happily ever after. Both share a deep and inexplicable fear of clowns. If they could have sex with any celebrity, both would choose Christina Hendricks. And both found themselves flummoxed by the games people played.

    MOLLY enters on Mark's side; LUCY enters Ally's side.

For Mark, that meant a woman who seemed perfectly normal might not be all she appeared.

MARK: I had a really nice time, Molly. I hope to see you soon.

    He shakes her hand. A long beat. MOLLY won't let go of his hand.

MOLLY: So... what? That's it?

MARK: Sorry?

MOLLY: What kind of a line is that? "See you soon?" Are you blowing me off, is that what you think you're doing? I mean, who the fuck do you think you are? You think you're so great? You think you're Dane Freaking Cook or something? Not by a longshot, buddy! You think you can just toss me aside after everything we shared—

MARK: Everything we shared? It was coffee!

MOLLY: Oh, God... I did it again, didn't I? I'm so stupid, so stupid! I'm sorry Mark, please forgive me! Let's just forget this ever happened, okay? Ha-ha! I had a really nice time, too. I hope to see you soon, too! See, it's all good! Happy times, happy times! I'm a pretty girl! Such a pretty girl!

    She crumples into his arms. The lights rise on ALLY and LUCY, at a bar.

NARRATOR: For Ally, it meant never understanding why intelligent women had to play dumb.

ALLY: I know Max is the wrong guy. Gloria Steinem would kill me for admitting this... but I just don't want to be alone.

LUCY: Your argument is faulty. Steinem herself wrote in "Revolution from Within" that when companionship comes at the price of your own identity, it's a fallacy. You are more alone than ever.

    A GUY approaches.

GUY: Excuse me. I bought you a drink.

    LUCY's entire demeanor changes.

LUCY: Ohmygawd, like, you paid for my drink? That is so cool, like, yeah! One sec!

A KIND OF LOVE STORY

LUCY (CONT'D) *(to Ally):* Furthermore, I would posit that Betty Friedan was correct when she said, "Every woman's prince is on the horizon, but only after they clear their head of the rogue."

GUY: Here, I got you a hurricane.

LUCY: Ohmygawd, what is it?

GUY: It's vodka and—

LUCY: No, I don't mean the drink! Like, really, what is a hurricane?

ALLY: Lucy, you're a meteorologist—

LUCY glares at her, then:

LUCY: Whoops, my hand slipped! I am such an airhead!

She knocks ALLY down. They all exit as the lights dim, then rise on DIANE and MARK, entering a theatre.

NARRATOR: For once, Mark had a date he knew couldn't go wrong. Diane was eager to check out the 25th anniversary screening of "The Princess Bride", and had asked Mark to accompany her.

DIANE: Oh, those! Grab those seats!

MARK: "As you wish!" Man, this is really exciting. I can't believe Bob didn't want to come. I can't imagine anyone not wanting to be here. It's totally—

MARK & DIANE: Inconceivable!

They chuckle.

DIANE: Oh you know how he is. He said no self-respecting straight man would be caught dead at "The Princess Bride."

MARK: Ah.

DIANE: I mean... well, you know. Um... oh look, the movie's starting!

The lights dim as the film starts.

All I meant was... I just don't want to be one of those women who forces a man to sit through a chick flick against their will.

MARK: Are you crazy? What kind of a jerk has to be dragged to "The Princess Bride"?

MAX enters, groaning and looking miserable. His arms are loaded with food. ALLY is right behind him.

ALLY: I told you we'd be late! Why'd you have to finish that Ms. Pac Man game?

MAX: Ally, I was almost done with level three, you know what that means! You get to see the stork drop off the baby! Come on, there's some seats.

MAX begins to enter the row behind MARK, stepping over several people in the process. At least ALLY looks embarrassed.

Pardon me, 'scuse me, hot stuff coming through!

He drops his popcorn bucket right on MARK.

MAX (CONT'D): Awww man! That was $12.50!

ALLY: I'm so sorry. Max, just sit down!

They sit. MAX begins sipping his drink. Then shaking his cup. The ice rattles loudly. MARK is growing irritated.

MAX: Ohhh yeah, Robin Wright. Robin Wright Now! I'd like to deflower her Buttercup, am I right?

Several SHHHHs.

ALLY: Max, quiet!

MAX: Wait, who's that guy? I thought Wesley was dead. What did he just say? Wait, what did he say when I asked what did he just say?

More SHHHs. ALLY is increasingly embarrassed.

MARK: Please, can you be quiet!

MAX: Soorrrrrry! *(Beat)* I'm not following this at all. Therefore, it is stupid.

He sneaks a beer out of his jacket. When it makes a sound as he opens it and ALLY glares at him, he makes his own "Sssst" sound. He guzzles it and drops it on the floor. Then: his phone rings. He answers it.

Go for Max! Nah, it's cool, I'm not doing anything—

EVERYONE begins shouting at MAX.

It's an important call! *(As he is exiting)* So, what are you wearing?

NARRATOR: As Mark and Diane reveled in the adventures of true love, swordplay, avenged fathers and ROUSes, Ally watched her favorite movie by herself. And yet it wasn't so bad; for she was beginning to realize that the times she felt the loneliest were when Max was right beside her.

The lights slowly dim to black. The music fades out.

The lights rise as everyone exits the theatre. MAX is loitering outside after the film; he spots MARK and DIANE.

MAX: Hey, neighbor! Fancy seeing you here.

He begins groping DIANE.

DIANE: Oh, hi Max. Mark, this is my neighbor. Max, this is—

MARK: We've met, actually.

MAX: Right, at the bar. Matt, right?

MARK: Mark.

MAX: You sure? Coulda sworn you said Matt.

DIANE: Max, I have to admit, I'm surprised to see you here. You come alone?

MAX: Nah, my girlfriend is in the bathroom, crying her eyes out.

MARK: I don't blame her. *(Catches self)* I mean... the ending of the movie always gets me too.

MAX: You're kidding, right? If you're a guy and you see "The Princess Bride" for any reason other than to get laid, you've gotta be a schmuck. Seriously, aren't you a little old to believe in this junk?

> *ALLY enters, catching the last bit of conversation.*

MARK: Maybe it is silly to get caught up in this stuff. I guess I never saw it that way. I never wanted to give up the hope there might be one person out there who was absolutely perfect for you, and you alone. I just never wanted to live in a world where believing love could conquer all was a bad thing. But maybe you're right. I'm a real schmuck.

DIANE: See you around, Max.

> *They exit. MAX takes a moment before he realizes ALLY is behind him.*

MAX: There you are. You done? I can't have you crying in public, people will get the wrong idea and think I'm a jerk or something. Ready to go?

ALLY: Max... I don't think this is working.

> *As MARK and ALLY return home:*

NARRATOR: If there was one thing Mark and Ally had learned, it was that happy endings don't come easy. The hero and the princess had so many obstacles to get past before they got their happily ever after. What neither one could have known at that moment, was that the wait was almost over.

> *MARK and ALLY start to turn towards each other...*
>
> *Blackout.*

SCENE 8

TITLE CARD – "CHAPTER SEVEN: ALL IN THE TIMING"

Melancholy music plays in the blackness. The lights rise as MARK and ALLY enter.

NARRATOR: Mark and Ally are two people with a long history of never getting the guy or girl. If they owned a carnival, it would have a Tunnel of Just Friends. When they were 10 years old, both dressed up for Halloween as Max from "Where the Wild Things Are." And both were hopeless when it came to understanding sexual politics.

CHARLOTTE enters on Mark's side; LUCY and two MEN enter on Ally's side.

For Mark, that meant every girl he met could only see him as a friend.

CHARLOTTE: You're going to find the right girl someday, Mark. I mean, you're smart, handsome, generous— you're a total catch! Any girl would be lucky to be with you.

MARK: Really? Would you want to go out sometime?

CHARLOTTE: Oh, no, you're not my type.

MARK: Ah. *(Trying to joke)* So I guess you go for dumb, ugly, selfish guys then?

CHARLOTTE *(no trace of humor)*: See? You get it!

ALLY is with LUCY at a bar; two men, COLIN and VICTOR, flank them.

NARRATOR: For her part, Ally couldn't understand why men found her roommate Lucy so fascinating.

ALLY: So it's not on the market yet and I really shouldn't reveal this, but my cousin has actually invented a pill that will eliminate the need for sleep—

LUCY: Ohmygawd I love inventing things! Like I chipped a nail but I made a replacement out of Scotch tape and a red Sharpie!

COLIN: You did? Let me see! My God, how did you even think of that??

LUCY: It's a gift!

ALLY: Yeah, so he's been working closely with the government and he learned that JFK's real assassin was—

LUCY: Ohmygawd, JFK! When I went to rent that movie, guess what they gave me?

VICTOR COLIN: What??   Tell us!

LUCY: A free candy bar! Isn't that crazy?

VICTOR: No way! Free???

COLIN: That's the most amazing thing ever!

ALLY *(shouting)*: I know Banksy's real identity!

A KIND OF LOVE STORY

A pause. They all look at her. VICTOR pushes her down. COLIN goes to help her up.

COLIN: Here, let me help you—

LUCY: First one to buy me a drink gets my phone number! Second one gets my panties!

COLIN drops ALLY as they all chase after LUCY. EVERYONE exits as Ally goes to her apartment.

NARRATOR: Perhaps it was because she was so confused by the opposite sex that Ally had been unable to sever ties from her awful boyfriend, Max Brockman.

MAX enters.

Having recently read several self-help books, he had become an expert at twisting everything she said.

ALLY: I'm sorry, Max. I just don't think this is working out.

MAX: Well, maybe you're just not trying hard enough. But I'm committed to making this work.

ALLY: I just... think that we want different things.

MAX: Well, all I want is a happy, healthy relationship based on mutual respect. If that's not what you want, I don't think I'm the one with the problem. Don't sabotage yourself, Ally. You deserve happiness.

ALLY: But Max—

MAX: You know, that cheesecake you made is fantastic. I'm going to get us a couple slices.

He checks out her ass.

Hm. Maybe just a half slice for you.

ALLY: Max!

MAX: What! I complimented your cooking! Why can't you focus on the positive?

He exits into the kitchen as LUCY enters.

LUCY: Well, you probably don't want to hear this... but he's kind of right.

ALLY: What do you mean?

LUCY: It's not easy out there, you know? Yes, he's not perfect. But it just seems like you're so quick to dispose of him without any real reason.

MAX re-enters, with cheesecake and a carrot.

MAX: Hey honey, I'm worried you're not getting enough vitamins, so I brought you some veggies instead. You're welcome.

ALLY: Max, we'll have to talk later. I'm late for my interview.

LUCY: That's right. Ally has a date with a lesbian tonight!

ALLY: Casey Collins is a feminist author who happens to be gay, yes. Her new book is amazing. It's all about how ridiculous gender stereotypes are.

LUCY: Hey, I'm not judging. I had my lesbian phase, too.

ALLY: Really? How long did that last?

LUCY: Fifteen years and counting!

MAX: Pfff... lesbians. There's no such thing. You show me a lesbian, I'll show you a woman who just hasn't met me yet. She'll change her mind when I take her to the gun show.

MAX kisses his biceps. ALLY just stares.

ALLY: Yeah, okay. Let's talk later.

MAX: Okay, Ally, just remember... you may not believe it, but you are just as worthy of love as anyone else.

MAX gives her a reassuring hug as the lights fade. Lights rise on MARK in his apartment as DIANE enters, visibly upset.

NARRATOR: While Ally was spending her night with an accomplished author and activist, Mark was surprised to find his evening interrupted by another remarkable woman. Bob had finally broached the subject with her about seeing other people, and sweet, loving Diane was upset.

DIANE: Motherfucking cocksucking needledick fuckface! *(Beat)* Balls!

NARRATOR: Really upset. And so she had gone to her oldest and dearest friend for comfort. And alcohol. Lots and lots of alcohol.

MARK hands her a flask, which she chugs. She finishes it off and hands it back to him.

MARK: Feel better?

DIANE: I'm sorry, Mark. I'm sure you have better things to do with your Friday night.

MARK: Sadly, I do not.

DIANE: This is like college all over again, isn't it? Bob and I have some stupid fight, and you stay up all night making me feel better.

MARK: Yes. Although asking for permission to cheat is a little more serious than losing your favorite Bananarama CD.

DIANE: Oh, that was a cruel summer, indeed.

They both sort of laugh as the lights fade and rise on ALLY, meeting CASEY at a café.

NARRATOR: Ally rarely found herself intimidated when on interviews, but Casey Collins was the kind of woman everyone either wanted or wanted to be. She had recently published her third book, "Sleeping Beauty Wakes," about antiquated ideas of love and sex in the modern age. If anyone asked, her favorite movie was "The Hours." It was actually "The Hangover." Two.

ALLY: So how did your parents react when you came out?

CASEY: Confused. My mom's exact words were: "But you're too pretty to be a lesbian." My brother was great about it, though. He was glad at least one of us was scoring with all the cheerleaders.

ALLY: So you had someone on your side.

CASEY: He couldn't be more supportive. I'm staying with him while I'm in town and he's even helping me throw the Sleeping Beauty Ball in honor of my book. Are you coming?

ALLY: Sleeping Beauty Ball?

CASEY: Basically a big costume ball where we all dress up like our favorite characters from fairy tales. Right up your alley. I read your column on the genesis of the Cinderella myth, it was fascinating.

ALLY: You've read my stuff?

CASEY: Of course, that's why I'm here. You're really good.

ALLY: You don't know what that means to me— I mean, you're sort of my role model. I want to be like you! In some ways, I mean. Like, you know, writing... and stuff. *(Beat)* I'm not gay. You probably knew that.

CASEY: Well, I figured, I mean, I hadn't seen you at the meetings.

ALLY: I'd like to be. I mean, sometimes I think it would be easier. That probably sounds really insulting, I didn't mean it like that. I just have a really lousy boyfriend, he doesn't get me at all and he doesn't even read my column which I know shouldn't be a big deal but wouldn't you be interested in what your significant other was saying and sometimes I just think I'd be better off with a woman but oh my God Ally, shut up!

CASEY: So if this guy is so lousy, why are you with him?

ALLY: My roommate says I have no good reason to not be with him.

CASEY: She sounds like a stepsister.

ALLY: A what?

CASEY: There's princesses and there's stepsisters. We all know what the princesses are about; they find the happily ever after. We don't know much about the stepsisters, other than they exist to fuck things up for the princesses. But I happen to take a sympathetic view of the stepsister. Imagine if you never found true love and had to watch as everyone around them does. Wouldn't it make you a little bitter?

ALLY: I suppose so.

> *The lights fade and rise on Mark's apartment. DIANE is leaning on MARK'S shoulder.*

DIANE: Is it me? Am I somehow not enough?

MARK: Diane, no. You know it's Bob, he's going through some mid-mid-life crisis. You're perfect.

DIANE: Perfect?

MARK: Sure. I mean, you've pretty much ruined my dating life. Every girl I meet has a tall order to fill. You're smart and funny and generous— you're the whole package. I mean, you set the standard. And the crazy part is, you don't even know it. That's what makes you you.

DIANE: Mark...

> *She kisses him. After a moment, he pulls away. They're both flustered.*

MARK: I'm sorry—

DIANE: No, I'm sorry. That was so unfair of me, you didn't ask for that, you didn't want that—

MARK: Diane, no. Believe me, I've thought about kissing you pretty much every day for the last 10 years. Just... just not like this. I can't.

DIANE: And that's what makes you you.

> *She nods, and rests her head on his shoulder as the lights fade. They rise on CASEY and ALLY; Casey is mid-thought while Ally is distracted.*

CASEY: So for years, my mom was convinced she "turned" me gay by letting me play Tom Sawyer in the third grade play. Ally? You okay?

ALLY: What if I'm a stepsister? What if I'm just destined to watch everyone around me fall in love and never find anyone myself? How do I keep from growing bitter? I mean, what if it's just not meant to happen for me?

> *ALLY is near tears. CASEY goes to comfort her.*

CASEY: Oh, Ally, no. I don't believe that. You are special. Anyone can see that just from looking at you. I promise you, I promise... you are going to find someone. Someone who reads you every day. Someone who sees what I see. Someone who'll move mountains for you. Because that's what you deserve. Someone who'll make you feel like the luckiest woman alive. But the truth is, they'll be the lucky one.

> *ALLY impulsively kisses her. After a moment, CASEY pulls away.*

Ally, you're amazing. But you're also hopelessly straight.

ALLY: I'm sorry, I just—

CASEY: Don't be sorry; I'm incredibly flattered. I'm just not up for converting straight girls. I've already met my quota for the month.

ALLY: It's just that everything about you makes sense to me. Why is that?

CASEY: Ally, there is someone out there for you. You're not silly to keep dreaming. And I'll do whatever I can to help that dream come true.

ALLY: Like my fairy godmother?

CASEY: Yeah, we're not crazy about that word.

> *The lights fade. They rise on Ally, as she returns home.*

A KIND OF LOVE STORY

NARRATOR: That night, Mark and Ally thought about how they had spent too much of their lives kissing the wrong people. And while it could make for a nice distraction, they had to believe there was something real waiting for them. And that the sweetest words they would ever hear were still waiting to be said.

> *ALLY walks into her apartment. MAX is there, in a state of undress.*

ALLY: Max? What are you doing here?

MAX: Ally! I was... waiting for you, of course. Why else would I be here?

> *LUCY enters, dressed provocatively and carrying a can of Crisco.*

LUCY: Okay, Loverboy, ready to see through time?

> *She stops at the sight of ALLY.*

Ally...! Okay, don't go jumping to conclusions.

> *ALLY is stunned into silence.*

NARRATOR: At times like this, when everything she thought she knew and believed was thrown back in her face, when her deepest trusts were betrayed, when the life she thought was set out in front of her was shattered... at such a time, there was really only one thing Ally could do.

> *ALLY starts laughing uncontrollably. She can't stop. LUCY and MAX just look scared.*

ALLY: Thank you! Thank you so much! Both of you, really! *(To Max)* We are so done. There is no reason for me to keep you in my life. *(Starts to exit; to Lucy)* You either.

> *She practically hugs them as she laughs and exits. They just stare at each other. (They're no longer into it now.)*

NARRATOR: Sometimes people say that when you least expect it, love happens. Sometimes they say that the moment you put the wrong person behind you is the moment the universe sends you the right person. And sometimes... they're right.

> *The lights rise as CASEY enters Mark's apartment.*

CASEY: Hey, little brother. Have I found the girl for you.

> *Blackout.*

SCENE 9

TITLE CARD – "CHAPTER EIGHT: EVER AFTER"

Melancholy music plays in the blackness. The lights rise as MARK and ALLY enter.

NARRATOR: Mark and Ally were both good people who had wasted too much time chasing bad love. Both had watched the YouTube video of the French bulldog who can't roll over at least a hundred times. Both preferred to live in an alternate reality where "LA Confidential" won the Oscar over "Titanic." And both had recently come to the realization that they deserved much better.

LUCY enters Mark's side while STEFAN enters Ally's side.

LUCY: Hey, Matt!

MARK: My name is Mark. Always has been, always will be.

LUCY: Whatever you say. Look, I was thinking I didn't really give you much of a chance on our last date. I mean, we hadn't even discussed your yearly salary and I just kind of flew out of there. But recent events have taught me maybe I need to be a little less picky and not get so hung up on looks, you know? So how about I give you another shot tonight?

MARK: I don't think so, Lucy.

LUCY laughs, long and hard.

LUCY: No, but seriously. Meet me at 8.

MARK: That's okay.

LUCY: Should we make it 9? You can even pick me up, providing you drive an S-class or higher.

MARK: Lucy, I don't want to be rude. But you're the most selfish, boorish, shallow person I've ever met. And I live in Los Angeles. How do I put this gently? I wouldn't date you if you swapped bodies with Angelina Jolie and offered to ride me all the way to the Kentucky Derby, because I would still have to listen to your idiotic braying. Have a nice day.

As he exits:

LUCY: But... I'm pretty!

The lights fade and rise on ALLY, listening to a jackass named STEFAN.

STEFAN: Well, look, normally I wouldn't do this, but it's pretty slim pickings here tonight, so how about I buy you a drink? Or would you just prefer the money?

ALLY: Ah... you are a smooth one, I'll give you that.

STEFAN: Let's be realistic here because I don't believe in mincing words. I'm a little out of your league but I'm willing to be generous if I drink enough. Why don't you come back to my place in Malibu? Oh, do you know where that is?

ALLY: Oh, look, I really appreciate the offer, but since you don't believe in mincing words, I'm going to return the favor. I could totally go home with you tonight to your ridiculously overpriced Malibu bachelor pad you can't even afford but need to hold onto because Daddy was never proud of you. I could even rock your world—and believe me, I would because girls like me know how to do things the bulimic mannequins you like to date because you're secretly terrified the world will see your obvious homosexuality would never do. But the truth is, "So You Think You Can Dance" is on tonight and you're just not worth TIVOing it for. Okay?

> *STEFAN is stunned. As ALLY starts to walk away, all he can muster is:*

STEFAN: Well... you're... bitch!

> *ALLY turns back around and sizes him up. After a second, she pushes him down.*

ALLY: Wow! That feels good! I get why people do it now!

> *EVERYONE exits. Lights rise on Mark's apartment: DIANE is on the couch with CASEY. Diane holds a copy of Casey's book. MARK enters, carrying his costume for the ball and a newspaper.*

NARRATOR: Mark's surge in confidence could be credited to recent developments in his personal life. And opportunities he had chosen not to take.

MARK: Hey, how's it going?

DIANE: Good. Your sister was just explaining to me how all men break down into Disney types. I've decided Bob is being a real Gaston.

MARK: Excellent. I just got my costume for tonight; I think everything is taken care of.

CASEY: Thanks for working your ass off, little brother. It's going to be a great night.

MARK: I think you're right. Did you see today's article? It's great publicity. And it really captured who you are.

CASEY: Yeah, I was pretty happy with it. The writer was really cool.

DIANE: Who was it?

MARK: Allison O'Neal. She's good, I read her column every week. She's... weird. In the best possible way.

CASEY: Okay, I better get started. I have a corset to wrestle.

DIANE: Thanks, Casey.

> *As CASEY exits, DIANE and MARK regard each other shyly.*

Thanks again for letting me stay here.

MARK: Oh come on, you know you're always welcome.

DIANE: You've been so great, Mark. And this is so embarrassing.

MARK: You have nothing to be embarrassed about.

DIANE: My husband just basically told me I'm not enough for him. And then I kiss you—

MARK: I enjoyed the kiss. Please don't apologize for it.

DIANE: You did?

MARK: Of course. It was everything I'd always dreamed it would be. But Diane... we're just... too late, you know? And I think I needed to realize that. Also, despite everything... you're still in love with Bob.

DIANE: I am. Dammit.

MARK: And he loves you too. He's left me 8 messages, looking for you. I'm sure he's called you at least 30 times.

DIANE: 39. I want to talk to him, but I can't. It just makes me crazy, you know? Thinking about him, living it up, while I'm here crying over him like an idiot.

> *The lights fade. "All By Myself" is playing as the lights rise on BOB in his apartment. He is a mess, slouched dejectedly in a chair with the phone in his hand. Bob picks up the phone to check that it's working.*

BOB: Hello? Hello?

> *He sighs and hangs it up. MAX enters the apartment.*

MAX: Bobby! How's the swinging bachelor lifestyle so far?

BOB: You! You're the devil who convinced me I was missing out by being with just one woman! You're Satan in a Members Only jacket!

MAX: Heyyyy! What's the matter? Aren't you enjoying singlehood?

BOB: What are you talking about? After I told Diane I wanted to see other people, she ran out of here crying. I've been trying to find her ever since. How could I hurt the sweetest, most giving woman in the world? ONE SECOND! *(Picks up phone)* Hello?

MAX: The phone didn't ring, Bob.

BOB: I have to keep checking! What if she's about to hang up after the first ring and I miss her? What if she doesn't come back? Look at me— it's been one day and I'm filthy as a Frenchman! What if I've messed things up for good? *(Checks phone)* Hello??

MAX: Look, you're just having doubts because you haven't been out there and seen all the great tail there is.

BOB: Yeah, you know what occurred to me the second she left? No one's better than Diane. If you're lucky enough to find someone who'll put up with you and all your stupid habits, you hang on to them. Don't let them get away. ONE SECOND! *(Checks phone)* HELLO?

A KIND OF LOVE STORY

MAX: Look, my friend is going to make you feel better about everything. She's the perfect girl— she's sexy, blonde, and has low self-esteem! Lucy!

LUCY enters, on the prowl. She makes a beeline for BOB.

LUCY: Is this Bob? You said above average.

MAX: I meant his income.

LUCY: Ooh! Great! *(To Bob)* Uh-oh, someone looks a little down! But Nurse Lucy has the cure for that! How about a massage?

MAX: You two kids have fun. I'll check in on you later.

MAX goes to exit as LUCY begins aggressively trying to undress BOB, who is trying to get away. She pulls his shirt over his head so he gets stuck in it.

Oh, and Bob: you're welcome!

The lights fade on Bob's apartment and rise on Kelly's. KELLY is helping ALLY get into her princess gown for the evening.

NARRATOR: While Lucy was making new friends, Ally had found herself with a new roommate. She had been taken in by her friend Kelly, the only woman who hated Max more than her.

ALLY is dozing off. KELLY shakes her awake.

KELLY: Are you falling asleep on your feet? I always thought that was just an expression.

ALLY: I'm exhausted. I can't believe I'm going anywhere tonight. But I promised.

KELLY: You look gorgeous. Any man would be a fool not to fall in love with you tonight.

ALLY: I think I'm taking a break from all that. What I want just isn't out there right now.

KELLY: And what is that?

ALLY: Someone who chooses the unusual. Who likes the mutt over the purebred. A guy who thinks Peter Jackson's best movie is "The Frighteners," not "Lord of the Rings." You know, a guy who, when you mention Herman Melville, doesn't go right to "Moby Dick" but brings up "Bartleby."

KELLY: Did you get all this from that Sleeping Beauty book?

ALLY: You have to read it. I'd lend it to you, but I left my copy with Lucy. Maybe she'll actually get something out of it.

KELLY: Lucy doesn't strike me as someone who knows how to... how do I say this... read.

There's a knock at the door. KELLY goes to get it.

ALLY: Too bad, she might figure out why she's so unhappy if she gave it a chance.

KELLY returns with a visibly nervous MAX.

KELLY: Hey, Ally. Looks like I win the bet. She thought it would take you two days to come crawling back. I said that with your lack of integrity, it would be less.

MAX: Well, I don't know what that word means, but I'm sure it's not a compliment.

KELLY *(to Ally)*: All this and brains, too. How do you resist?

MAX: Kelly, I know you don't like me—

KELLY laughs.

But I have something I need to say to Ally. And I'm not leaving until I say it.

KELLY *(to Ally)*: You okay with this?

ALLY: It's fine.

KELLY starts to exit.

MAX: I'm not afraid of you!

KELLY turns and hisses at him; MAX shrieks like a little girl. She laughs and exits. Max looks at ALLY.

(Off the outfit)

You going out?

ALLY: No, just staying in tonight. What do you want, Max? I have a costume ball and I'm late.

MAX: So look... none of us are perfect. We've both made mistakes. Let's be adults and move past this.

ALLY: Is that... an apology?

MAX: Hey, hey, let's not go throwing around words like "apology" or "fault." Let's just agree we're both to blame.

ALLY: I was a great girlfriend. I would have done anything to make you happy. You cheated on me with my roommate and a can of Crisco.

MAX: Yeah, but I don't even like her!

ALLY: So???

MAX: So it doesn't count!

ALLY: Max... I'm so over you. It's not going to happen.

She brushes past him to exit. He calls to her:

MAX: What, you think you can do better? You think you're going to get the white knight on the horse to carry you away? It doesn't happen Ally, not for girls like you.

Stung; she takes a moment. Finally:

ALLY: You know, Max, one day you're going to meet your match. You're going to find someone you're crazy about. And she's going to break your heart.

A KIND OF LOVE STORY

ALLY (CONT'D): And you're going to finally realize how horribly you treated me all this time. And you're going to feel really bad about it. I just want you to know... that I forgive you.

> *She exits. The lights rise in Mark's apartment. He and CASEY are dressed for the party. DIANE takes a photo of them together.*

DIANE: You guys look great.

MARK: You sure you won't come?

DIANE: Oh, no... I wouldn't be good company tonight. But have a great time.

CASEY: Oh, Mark, I need you to pick up one more thing before the party.

> *She hands him a note.*

Here's the address.

MARK: What is it?

CASEY: You'll know it when you see it. See you there.

> *She exits. As she heads out the door, she bumps into BOB. He's a mess— his shirt is on backwards/inside out and he is panicked.*

Oh! Hello!

BOB: Hi, sorry, excuse me— Mark?

> *He brushes past CASEY, who shrugs and exits.*

Mark, you're not returning my calls, I need to talk to you—

> *He spots DIANE.*

Diane! You're here! Oh my God, are you okay?

DIANE: What are you doing here?

BOB: Me? I came to talk to Mark— what are you doing here? Wait. What's going on?

DIANE: Hey! You don't get to play the jealous husband! You were the one who wanted a break!

BOB: Yes, but only because I'm an idiot! Diane, the second you left I knew what a fool I'd been. I don't want anyone else. And when it comes down to it, I can't be with anyone else. A very scary lady taught me that.

DIANE: Bob, I don't want you to come back to me just because you don't think you can do any better.

BOB: It's not that. It's that when you're gone, for even a minute, I miss you. I want to share everything that happens with you. I know I've been a jerk. I got this stupid idea in my head, but that's all it was, an idea. And you're always so understanding, it never occurred to me that I would hurt you. When I actually said it out loud, I felt like such a fool. Diane, there is no one else for me. It's only you. It's always been you.

> *DIANE softens. She looks to MARK.*

DIANE: Am I an idiot for believing this? Or do you think he means it?

MARK: I think he means it. And I think you deserve Paris.

> *He kisses her forehead and exits. DIANE, still resistant, turns to BOB.*

BOB: I know I don't deserve it... but if you give me a chance, I want to spend the rest of my life making it up to you. I want to... I want to know how I can make you happy. What were your hopes and your dreams, before you made a life with me? What is it you want?

DIANE: I thought... I thought you'd never ask.

> *They kiss. The lights rise on ALLY entering a room. She checks her notes, looks around. She sits on the couch.*

ALLY: Hello?

NARRATOR: When Ally arrived at the address Casey had given her for the party, she was already exhausted from an emotional day. So she really didn't mind that she seemed to be the only one in the empty warehouse, she could use the time to collect her thoughts. And as the minutes ticked by, she relaxed more and more.

> *ALLY leans back on the couch. She closes her eyes.*

Perhaps too much. It was beginning to look like Ally might miss the party— and, once again, her destiny— altogether.

> *After a moment, MARK enters. He looks around. Spots ALLY. Makes his way to her. A beat. Confused, Mark leans over to look at her... studies her. Suddenly, her eyes fly open.*

ALLY: Oh!

MARK: Sorry! Sorry! I didn't mean to wake you!

ALLY: No— sorry, I was just resting my eyes. It's been a crazy few days and I haven't slept much and I'm staying with a friend on the most uncomfortable couch... what time is it?

MARK: Almost 8. I'm sorry... this sounds like the most ridiculous line but... do I know you?

ALLY: I think... you might. You look familiar to me too.

MARK: I'm Mark... Collins.

ALLY: I'm Ally. O'Neal.

MARK: O'Neal? Like Allison O'Neal, the writer?

ALLY: Okay, someone put you up to this, right? You recognize my name? I mean, I'm not exactly Herman Melville.

MARK: Too bad, because I love Bartleby. No, I read your column. Every day. And you... you just did a piece on Casey Collins. She's my sister.

ALLY: Wait. You're Casey's brother? The amazing, understanding, helpful brother she's staying with?

MARK: Yes, but most people just call me Mark.

ALLY: You're the one throwing her party— or is this just a bold fashion choice?

MARK: No, I'm throwing the party.

ALLY: Where is the party? Am I early?

MARK: What do you mean? It's at the warehouse downtown.

ALLY: Casey told me it was here— this is the address she gave me.

MARK: No, its downtown, always has been.

ALLY: Then what are you doing here?

MARK: She asked me to pick something up—

He catches himself.

Ah.

ALLY: Oh. My fairy godmother.

MARK: This must seem hopelessly cheesy to you.

ALLY: No. I mean, I'm not one to judge. I'm the girl who cries at "Armageddon."

MARK looks at her, surprised.

MARK: Well, how can you not...

MARK & ALLY: I mean, when Will Patton's kid sees him on TV—

They both stop and look at each other, startled.

MARK: Look, I'm more than happy to take you to the ball if you want. You look so stunning, it shouldn't go to waste. Or if you feel like it, we could always go get a drink. You know, alcohol. Or coffee. Coffee is a nice, legal narcotic. I'm rambling now, aren't I? I'm sorry.

ALLY: No, it's fine. Really. I would love to.

MARK: You would?

ALLY: Well, how could I say no to someone in that outfit? I mean, it seems like we're kind of made for each other, aren't we?

MARK: Yeah. Okay. Great. Shall we?

He offers his hand. She takes It and they start to walk off together...

ALLY: Mark... I know we just met, but I think I have to warn you. I've been through a lot and I'm not up for playing games or hiding my feelings or any of that stuff. So just so you know... If you ever fuck with me, I'll hurt you.

MARK: Ally, if I ever fucked with you, I'd hurt myself.

ALLY: Wow. Good answer.

They begin to stroll about.

NARRATOR: As Mark and Ally spent the evening, talking, exploring and learning only a fraction of what they would come to find they had in common, both of them marveled at how right the evening felt. There was no effort, no discomfort, in their dialogue. They fell into an instant shorthand with one another. And as they cautiously celebrated how perfect it all felt, they believed once and for all in fate. Even so, they couldn't have known then how destiny would work out for the other people in lives.

BOB and DIANE appear in spotlight, cuddling.

BOB: I love you.

DIANE: I know. *(Beat)* I love you, too.

CASEY appears in a spotlight. LUCY approaches her, carrying her book.

LUCY: Excuse me? Miss Collins? I just... I wanted you to know how much your book meant to me. It came to me at a time in my life when... I really needed it.

CASEY: Aren't you kind. And beautiful! I'm Casey.

LUCY goes to shake her hand; CASEY kisses it.

LUCY: Lucy.

MAX enters KELLY's apartment in a rush.

MAX: Look, I don't know what you have against me =or what I ever did to you, but I don't care if you like me or not, okay? I mean, I'm not going to keep myself up at night caring what you think about me... anymore. Why should I let you have that effect on me? I mean, what is it about you that puts me so on edge?

A beat. KELLY grabs his face and kisses him. MAX is stunned. She starts to exit. He chases after her.

Kelly... wait!

EVERYONE exits, leaving MARK and ALLY alone onstage together. They look at each other, and go in to kiss.

NARRATOR: In the history of time, there have been many first kisses. Some weren't that memorable. Some were epic enough to start wars-

MARK and ALLY stop and look up to where the NARRATOR presumably is.

ALLY: Hey, you know what? I think we're okay now.

MARK: Yeah, we really appreciate everything you've done. But we'll take it from here. Thanks.

Silence. MARK and ALLY kiss. After a beat:

NARRATOR: This was the story of two people who were made for each other. A man and a woman destined to fall madly in love— who finally found each other.

Fade to black.

THE END

STEELE SPRING STAGE RIGHTS

ABOUT STAGE RIGHTS

Based in Los Angeles and founded in 2000, Stage Rights is one of the foremost independent theatrical publishers in the United States, providing stage performance rights for a wide range of plays and musicals to theater companies, schools, and other producing organizations across the country and internationally. As a licensing agent, Stage Rights is committed to providing each producer the tools they need for financial and artistic success. Stage Rights is dedicated to the future of live theatre, offering special programs that champion new theatrical works.

To view all of our current plays and musicals, visit:
www.stagerights.com

Made in the USA
Columbia, SC
03 November 2021